The Structure and Reform of the U.S. Tax System

The Structure and Reform of the U.S. Tax System

Albert Ando
Marshall E. Blume
Irwin Friend

The MIT Press
Cambridge, Massachusetts
London, England

© 1985 by The Massachusetts Institute of Technology

This book was set in Palatino by Achorn Graphic Services, Inc., and printed and bound by Halliday Lithograph Corp. in the United States of America.

Library of Congress Cataloging in Publication Data

Ando, Albert.
 The structure and reform of the U.S. tax system.

 Bibliography: p.
 Includes index.
 1. Tax incidence—United States. 2. Taxation—United States. I. Blume, Marshall. II. Friend, Irwin. III. Title.
HJ2322.A3A52 1985   336.2'05'0973   85-235
ISBN 0-262-01086-0

To our wives

Contents

List of Tables

Preface

This study was written by Albert Ando, Marshall E. Blume, and Irwin Friend under the general direction of Friend and Blume, director and associate director, respectively, of the Rodney L. White Center for Financial Research of the Wharton School of the University of Pennsylvania. We are grateful for the many helpful comments we received from our colleagues, Alan Auerbach and Paul Taubman of the University of Pennsylvania and Joseph Pechman of the Brookings Institution. Although our colleagues contributed greatly to the improvement of our manuscript, they do not necessarily agree with all of its contents.

Chapter 1 provides a summary of our main results. Chapter 2 describes the structure and incidence of the U.S. tax system as it exists at the time of this writing (December 1984). It corrects a number of common misconceptions. Contrary to popular belief income from capital is now taxed less heavily than income from labor. Also combining federal, state, and local taxes, the rich generally do not pay an appreciably higher proportion of their income in taxes than poorer groups.

Chapter 3 analyzes in some detail the economic as well as equity implications of the different major forms of taxation. On the basis of theory and empirical evidence, it points out that there is no strong scientific basis for believing that shifting income taxes from capital to labor or from the upper- to the lower-income groups would have a substantial long-run effect on saving or capital formation. Indeed such a shift might have a greater adverse impact on the labor supply than a beneficial effect on capital formation. Yet a general decrease in marginal tax rates might be expected to stimulate to some extent the economic activity being taxed. Moreover a more equal taxation of different household and business activities would contribute to allocational efficiency, economic growth, and the distributional equity of the tax burden.

Chapters 4, 5, and 6 deal with three major types of taxation: personal income taxes, corporate income taxes, and consumption taxes. Personal and, to a lesser extent, corporate income taxes (including social security taxes) are currently the major source of federal tax revenues. For some time substantial attention has been paid to congressional flat tax proposals, especially those by Senator Bill Bradley and Congressman Richard Gephardt and by Congressman Jack Kemp and Senator Bob Kasten. These proposals would greatly lower marginal tax rates on different income groups and at the same time broaden the tax base so as to maintain the same tax-income ratios for different income groups as currently. These proposals would also lower the marginal tax rates for corporations and at the same time reduce depreciation allowances and tax credits so as to maintain the same average tax rates as currently. These proposed congressional income tax reforms are analyzed at some length in this study, with some suggestions for improvement. This study also suggests an alternative mechanism, a gradual expansion of the minimum tax provisions in the current tax law for achieving more slowly the same objectives as the flat tax approach but perhaps with less political furor and fewer unforeseen transitional problems.

The concluding chapter examines the relative advantages and disadvantages of what would be for the United States two new forms of taxation: the value-added tax (VAT), which has been used extensively in Europe, and a comprehensive cash-flow tax, which has yet to be used successfully anywhere but has received substantial academic support in recent years. Both the VAT and cash-flow taxes are consumption-based taxes and would represent a substantial departure from the present tax structure in the United States, which is primarily based on income. Neither the VAT nor the cash-flow tax seems to have much legislative or administrative support at this time.

There is one obvious omission in this study's analysis of the major tax reforms proposed in recent years. In November 1984, the U.S. Department of the Treasury sent to the president a new flat tax proposal, which we have not had time to integrate into the body of this study. We shall, however, comment briefly here on the proposal. Since we have had access only recently to the summary and backup volumes of the Treasury Department's Report on Fundamental Tax Simplification and Reform, we are not in a position to discuss this proposal in detail.

The new Treasury proposal, like the other flat tax reforms discussed in our study, lowers marginal personal income tax rates substantially, especially at the top of the income distribution; reduces the number of tax brackets from seven to three (15 percent, 25 percent, and 35 percent); greatly increases the personal income tax base by modifying or repealing a number of itemized deductions, exclusions, and special tax credits; adjusts realized capital gains for inflation and then taxes the adjusted gains at the normal rather than preferential income tax rate; increases personal exemptions and zero bracket amounts to eliminate from taxation virtually all families with income below the poverty levels; lowers the corporate tax rate to 33 percent; repeals the corporate investment tax credit; reduces accelerated depreciation for many corporations but provides for inflation adjustments so that depreciation allowances for tax purposes are set to approximate economic depreciation; repeals the current tax exemption for new state and local government revenue bonds; and curtails other tax shelters.

From the viewpoint of economic efficiency, the Treasury proposal is in several important respects an improvement over the Bradley-Gephardt (B-G) and Kemp-Kasten (K-K) bills. These improvements include the taxation of employer-provided fringe benefits; several measures designed to prevent the abusive use of business deductions for personal consumption (such as expenditures for entertainment, holiday travel, and lavish meals); other measures to prevent the abusive use of trusts for children and similar devices for avoiding or minimizing taxation; the elimination of the federal income tax deduction for state and local income and other local taxes; the elimination of tax deductions for unrealized real gains on property contributed to charitable organizations; the provision of less generous allowances generally for charitable contributions; the introduction of a cap on nonmortgage personal interest payments that can be classed as an expense for tax purposes; the repeal of preferential tax treatment available to many financial institutions; and taking a significant step toward integration of the corporate and personal income taxes by allowing corporations to deduct half of dividends paid to stockholders from the company's taxable income.

Two other features of the Treasury proposal are clearly superior to those in B-G or K-K. First, the Treasury proposal in principle makes only the real component of interest income taxable for both individuals and corporations, and, symmetrically, only the real component of interest paid deductible, except for interest paid on mortgages on principal residences. This is a desirable feature and should be extended to mortgages on principal residences as well. Treasury also retains the general indexation of the zero-bracket amount, personal exemptions, and rate brackets that become effective January 1, 1985, under present law. This retention of the indexation provision in the present law is similar to the K-K but different from the B-G proposal. On the whole, such indexation is desirable.

Second, in order to reduce the availability of tax shelters, the Treasury proposal contains a provision that requires partnerships with more than thirty-five partners to be taxed as though they were corporations, thus prohibiting partnerships from passing on tax losses to individual partners. Although this may not be the best way to handle the vexing problem of such tax shelters, it does seem to be a fairly effective measure, and its presence clearly improves the overall quality of the Treasury proposal.

One respect in which the Treasury's proposal permits greater reduction in the tax base than the existing law or other major tax reform proposals is in its liberalization of individual retirement account (IRA) deductions. Another important respect in which Treasury would permit more liberal deductions than the B-G but not the K-K proposal is in its retention of the full mortgage interest deduction on owned homes permitted under present law.

Several of the provisions in the Treasury proposal will significantly reduce the bias in present law in favor of corporate debt and retained earnings at the expense of external equity financing and the bias in favor of the partnership form of organization at the expense of the corporate form. A number of the proposals would also result in significant windfall gains or losses in the transitional period, which the Treasury attempts to minimize through a number of different measures, including grandfathering income from old assets in certain instances and delayed or phased-in enactment dates in other cases. Thus the 50 percent dividend paid deduction would be fully phased in only by January 1, 1992.

Although we have not yet examined the basis for these calculations, the Treasury estimates that its proposal would be approximately tax neutral for all taxpayers combined, with a 25 percent increase in corporate taxes offset by an 8.5 percent cut in personal taxes. The Treasury also states that the proposal does not change the distribution of individual income taxes across most income classes, though it does reduce taxes more than proportionately for taxpayers with the lowest income, with an estimated average reduction of 32.5 percent for families with income below $10,000 and 16.6 percent between $10,000 and $15,000. If these estimates are approximately valid, the progressivity of the current tax structure would be moderately increased.

From the viewpoints of economic efficiency and equity, one major gap in the Treasury's proposal relates to its recommended tax treatment of capital gains, a deficiency it shares with the other flat tax proposals: no provision is made for the taxation of unrealized capital gains even at the time of death of the taxpayer. As our study points out, although it may not be practical to tax unrealized capital gains systematically as they accrue, there does not seem to be any justification for not taxing them at some convenient time, such as at death.

It might also be noted that although the indexation of realized capital gains as recommended by the Treasury may be desirable, indexation would make more sense if applied to the taxation of all capital gains, both realized and unrealized. Otherwise there may be an incentive for taxpayers to postpone realization on their more successful investments and use their less successful investments, which show tax losses when adjusted for inflation, as a basis for minimizing taxes. The taxation of unrealized capital gains at least at time of death would also add badly needed tax revenue without significant social or economic cost. We should like to point out, however, that the Treasury proposal, even without changes, would be a substantial improvement over current tax law.

Though the Treasury proposal was made public only very recently, with some of the support material not yet available, it already has been subject to major criticism by a number of groups which feel they would be adversely affected. The strongest criticism of general economic interest has come from business organizations, which claim that the elimination of several of the special business investment incentives described earlier would result in a major if not catastrophic decrease in business investment and hence in economic growth. However, as discussed at length in our study, while tax incentives may have a substantial short-run effect on business investment, there is no scientific evidence that they have a substantial long-run effect since they do not seem to increase significantly the overall rate of private saving. As a result any long-run tax-induced decrease in business investment associated with the elimination of these special incentives would be limited in size.

Finally, we point out a major deficiency in our study and in all the tax reforms proposed recently: they deliberately define their purpose as reforming the tax structure to make it simpler, more equitable, and more efficient while retaining the total taxes currently collected. Given the current and foreseeable unprecedented size of government deficits, the most urgent fiscal problem may well be how best to reduce the deficit through some combination of increases in taxes and decreases in government expenditures rather than to rationalize the structure of taxes. In its attempt to reform the tax structure, the government can ill afford to put the reduction of the deficit on the back burner.

The Structure and
Reform of the
U.S. Tax System

1   Introduction and Summary

Background of Study

Complaints about the level and structure of taxes have become increasingly widespread in the United States as both the level of taxes and the complexity of the tax system have increased. Associated with this increase in taxation and its complexity has been a growth in the unevenness of the tax burden on different households and on different business firms within any income group. This disparate tax treatment of different kinds of income and expenditure has resulted in economic inefficiencies and a widespread perception of unfairness.

This deep dissatisfaction with the tax system has led to a number of proposals for sweeping changes in the structure of federal taxes. Although there is no general agreement on how to make these changes, those receiving most attention among legislators, economists, and the press have been several variants of flat federal income taxes and, to a much lesser extent, two types of consumption taxes, a value-added tax (VAT) and a cash-flow consumption tax.

The best-known proposals for flat federal income taxes are those by Senator Bill Bradley and Congressman Richard Gephardt (B-G) and by Congressman Jack Kemp and Senator Bob Kasten (K-K). The key features of both proposals are a substantial reduction in the top marginal tax rates with reductions for individuals from 50 percent to 30 percent (B-G) or 25 percent (K-K) and for corporations from 46 percent to 30 percent.

Coupled with these reductions is the elimination or modification of enough of the special tax treatment of certain types of income and expenditures to retain approximately unchanged the total dollars of taxes, as well as their distribution among income groups. These special tax provisions, commonly called tax expenditures, have been estimated by the Joint Tax Committee at over $295 billion in fiscal 1983 and are projected under current law to amount to nearly $421 billion in fiscal 1988. These provisions include special provisions for exclusion of certain forms of income, deductions from gross income, special tax credits, preferential tax rates, and deferrable tax liabilities. In both years the committee's estimates exclude the tax loss from not taxing unrealized capital gains.

The initial purpose of the great bulk of these tax expenditures was to encourage or assist specific activities or groups, such as corporate pension plans, home owners, municipalities, and charitable organizations. To a much less important extent in terms of the amounts involved, some of these tax expenditures were enacted to make the tax structure more equitable, such as the tax deductions for two-earner married couples or for abnormal medical expenditures. For some tax expenditures, such as the favorable tax treatment of capital gains, both types of justification have been advanced: on the one hand, the desirability of encouraging investment in risky capital, and on the other hand, the desire to distinguish between inflation-induced and real capital gains.

The original emphasis on flat taxes was to lower marginal tax rates, provide additional incentives for saving, investment, and labor, diminish the distortions caused by special tax provisions, enhance equity among different tax-payers, and reduce economic inefficiencies. With the recent growing concern about the size of the government deficits even in periods of prosperity, however, the ability of flat tax proposals to raise revenue in future years without raising nominal tax rates has also received attention. The reason for this potentially favorable tax effect is that under current law the value of tax expenditures would increase more rapidly than gross tax revenues. Hence a flat tax that both lowered tax rates and reduced tax expenditures could produce positive net revenues (or lower deficits) in the future as revenues grow faster than expenditures.

As a basis for choosing among the different suggestions for major changes in the structure of taxes, this study considers in some detail the equity, efficiency, countercyclical, and transitional implications of proposed tax changes, with special emphasis on issues of equity and efficiency. To distribute the burden of taxes as equitably as possible, virtually everyone, except perhaps some special interest groups, agrees with the general principle of horizontal equity—that households (or businesses) with equivalent economic means should pay the same amount of taxes.

All of the flat tax proposals contain substantital reductions in tax expenditures that are designed to further this objective of horizontal equity. Although there is less of a consensus on how the burden of taxes should be distributed most equitably among different income groups, probably most people would agree that upper-income groups should pay at least as high a percentage of their income in taxes as lower-income groups. This principle, termed vertical equity, represents an ethical consideration. Economic considerations might, of course, argue for a different distribution of taxes from that based solely on equity considerations.

Incidence of Current Taxes

In 1966 federal, state, and local taxes in total were fairly progressive in that the ratio of total taxes to income increased with income. By 1985 this progressivity has largely disappeared, with an average tax rate of close to 25 percent paid by most income groups, including the top 1 percent of the population. Most of the decline in progressivity occurred between 1970 and 1975, with a more modest decline in the 1980–1985 period. This decline in the relative burden of taxes for the top income class is due mainly to a decline in the effective rates of capital gains taxes and corporate income taxes, an increase in payroll taxes falling largely on the lower-income groups, a decrease in the relative value of per capita exemptions, and, subsequent to 1980, a lower maximum marginal tax rate on individuals.

The ratio of direct and indirect taxes to total income within an income group is one important measure of the fiscal burden borne by these groups and is now relatively constant across income groups. There are limitations to this measure, and this study considers a number of alternative measures of tax incidence and fiscal burden. Of particular interest among these alternatives are the ratio of taxes to income adjusted for social welfare benefits or transfer payments and the ratio of taxes to wealth or net worth. The rate of taxation after adjusting for social welfare benefits and transfers is quite progressive currently, at least until the $20,000–50,000 level. On the other hand the ratio of taxes to wealth is strongly regressive for all wealth groups and would remain regressive for most groups even with the ratio adjusted for social welfare benefits and transfers.

The decline in progressivity of taxes over the past twenty years reflects both a decline in the progressivity of taxes on labor income and a marked reduction in the taxation of capital income. Upper-income groups tend to have a greater concentration of capital income and thus would benefit on average from this shift. The current heavier taxes on labor than on capital income represent a reversal of the relative tax burden in 1966.

Efficiency Issues

In addition to its direct incidence on different income and other groups in the population, the structure of taxes can affect the economy in many important ways. For example, the tax system can alter saving and investment behavior, the supply of labor, the level of the stock market, the functioning of other financial markets and institutions, the form and capital structure of business and investor portfolios, and ultimately the allocation of resources among industries. This study examines these characteristics of the tax structure, especially with respect to the level and growth of real economic activity. It does not address the important question of what are appropriate aggregate levels of taxes and government outlays.

Perhaps the most severe economic criticism of the U.S. tax structure over the past decade has been the alleged excess taxation of income on capital. Such taxation has been blamed for contributing importantly to a low ratio of saving and investment to the national income and hence to a low rate of economic growth. Implicit in such criticism is that, for a given total amount of tax revenue, more should come from the taxation of labor and less from that of capital. As a result of tax changes, however, capital income is no longer taxed more heavily than labor income, so that any further shift of taxation toward labor would have to balance carefully any beneficial effect on saving and capital formation against the detrimental effect on labor supply and on the distribution of taxes by income group.

The relevant theoretical and empirical evidence in the United States and, to a limited extent, in other countries gives no reason to believe that lower taxes on capital income would have any substantial, long-term effect in stimulating the private sector's propensity to save or the rate of capital formation. Although the level of taxes may not appreciably affect the overall rate of savings, the tax structure itself may have substantial impact on how savings are allocated.

It is possible, but far from certain, that a significant increase in capital formation could be brought about for some time by a large reduction in taxes on capital income, especially at the corporate level, but the long-run effect is probably quite limited because of the apparently low long-run after-tax interest elasticity of saving. Moreover if the reduction in taxes on capital income is offset by an increase in labor taxes, the incentives for labor would be reduced, with a possible adverse effect on the economy, and probably there would be a shift in the incidence of taxation from upper- to middle- and lower-income families. The available empirical evidence suggests that in the long run, labor may well be as sensitive to income taxes, if not more so, as saving and investment.

Taxes undoubtedly provide some disincentives to the economic activity being taxed, but there is no strong evidence that these disincentives in the aggregate are very substantial. Nonetheless it is desirable to reduce these disincentives. This can be done by minimizing to the extent possible the marginal rates of tax paid on income, keeping them consistent with the desired rate of progressivity in the average tax-income ratio. The flat tax proposals represent one approach to advancing this objective through the reduction of the marginal tax rates coupled with a broadening effect of the tax base to leave government revenues unchanged and through an increase in personal tax exemptions and deductions to maintain the same distribution of the tax burden by income groups as under the current system.

The substitution of flat or progressive consumption taxes for flat or progressive income taxes might stimulate aggregate saving moderately, at least in the short run and perhaps even longer. Consumption taxes might have a somewhat more stimulating effect on savings but also a larger adverse effect on labor incentives, although the magnitude of either effect is probably not great. A major advantage of a consumption tax is that it eliminates all direct taxes on capital income and thus would cause no distortion in how savings are invested. A major disadvantage of a consumption tax is that it is harder to control the incidence of taxes by income class.

Other taxes that would be expected to have less effect on saving and labor incentives than an income tax of comparable progressivity are the gift and inheritance taxes. These taxes, which have never yielded very large revenues in the United States, were reduced markedly in 1981. The effect was a decline in the incidence of taxes on the wealthy. Since consumption taxes tend to be more regressive than income taxes and to place less of a tax burden on wealth, it is even more important that any reform of the tax structure in the direction of consumption taxes should be integrated with a reform of gift and inheritance taxes.

The appropriate treatment of taxes on capital gains has posed some of the most controversial issues in taxation and is considered in some detail in this study. Historically capital gains have been taxed at extremely low rates. The effective rate of taxation on all capital gains is very much smaller than the rate on realized gains due to the fact that unrealized gains are never taxed if transferred at the death of the taxpayer or upon a donation to a tax-exempt institution. Thus in the past the effective rate on realized and unrealized capital gains combined is estimated to have been only about 5 percent.

A more appropriate basis for capital gains taxation would be to apply the much higher normal income tax rate to capital gains but with the basis adjusted for inflation. A full indexing scheme for the taxation of capital income would also exclude from taxation that portion of interest payments that is just compensation for inflation. The arguments for preferential treatment of capital gains are generally highly questionable even though there are real practical problems in taxing unrealized gains on a current basis. At a minimum it would appear that realized capital gains (adjusted for inflation) should be taxed at the same rate as ordinary income and that unrealized capital gains (again adjusted for inflation) should at least be taxed ultimately, such as at the time of death or other disposition.

The structure of taxation can affect the economy not only through effects on saving, investment, and labor supply but also through the allocation of resources to different economic activities. The preferential treatment of some forms of income encourages greater output of the favored activities at the expense of other activities. Thus current taxation favors housing, business equipment, state and local government outlays, and certain industries at the expense of other outlays and activities. Such differential tax treatments, frequently major in magnitude, generally lead to violation of horizontal equity and to inefficiencies in the allocation of resources.

Most economists would agree that except for compelling reasons of social policy, taxes should not be levied unevenly on different sources of incomes. Yet in 1982 the average effective tax rate on existing corporate capital varied among industries from 6.3 percent to 39.4 percent and was negative on new investment for several industrial groups. Only by totally exempting investment income from taxation, as in a consumption tax, could the tax system be neutral with respect to the allocation of resources, but a consumption tax carries with it its own special distributional and transitional problems.

The major flat tax proposals attempt to reduce greatly differential tax treatment for both individual and corporate taxpayers. They still retain some tax expenditure items for reasons of social policy, political feasibility, and perhaps also to ease transitional difficulties.

Individual Income Tax Reform

Proposals advanced recently for reforming the federal income tax structure share a number of common features. They eliminate many of the deduction and exclusion provisions, thus broadening the tax base and contributing to horizontal equity and economic efficiency. At the same time they reduce marginal tax rates appreciably over all income classes, especially at the upper levels. In order to offset the regressive shift in the tax burden associated with this reduction in marginal rates while generating the same level of revenues for the government, these proposals provide for an increase in personal exemptions and standard deductions in addition to broadening the tax base.

Most economists agree that the tax base should be broadened to the extent feasible by eliminating or greatly reducing virtually all special tax expenditures. One of the most serious omissions of the current proposals is their failure to provide for the taxation of unrealized capital gains. Although there are certainly some real practical difficulties in taxing unrealized capital gains, it should be recognized that unrealized capital gains are very large in size and constitute the great bulk of all capital gains. The tax system should tax unrealized capital gains at least at the time of the ultimate disposition of the asset. At death unrealized capital gains might be taxed either as income to the deceased or through inheritance taxes. For gifts the difference between the acquisition cost and the valuation of the gift should be imputed to the donor as income.

Another major base-broadening change many economists would find desirable is to treat both employees' and employers' contributions to the social security system as taxes and to allow them as tax credits or deductions against the tax base. In this case all benefits from the system would be included as income in the tax base of the beneficiaries. A first step in this direction was made in 1984 when half of the benefits were made taxable if the combined income of the household exceeds a specified amount ($25,000 for a single return or $32,000 for a joint return).

In general there is little economic basis for many, if not most, of the different tax expenditures. At times a special public policy objective is used to justify a specific tax benefit (for example, the desirability of encouraging home ownership or charity), but once we allow one exception, it becomes exceedingly difficult to deny another. In the elimination of a specific type of tax expenditure, however, as in all other major changes in the tax laws, there may be major transitional effects on particular groups in the population, and, if so, some consideration might be given to cushioning these impacts.

Of the two major recent proposals for tax reform, by Bradley-Gephardt and Kemp-Kasten, the study examines the first more closely than the second, mainly because of the greater wealth of data available to analyze the implications of the B-G proposal; however, the two proposals have the same major objectives and have many similar provisions for implementing them.

The B-G proposal for revising the individual taxes contains five major parts:

1. It eliminates or substantially decreases a large number of the special provisions that reduce the tax base, recover-

ing about $110 billion in tax revenues or roughly one-half of the dollar amount involved in the special tax expenditure items listed by the Joint Committee on Taxation.

2. Personal exemptions are increased to $1,600 for the taxpayer and spouse and remain at $1,000 for all other dependents. The standard deductions increase from $2,300 to $3,000 for single returns and from $3,400 to $6,000 for joint returns.

3. The regular tax rate will be 14 percent for all incomes, with surtaxes of 12 percent starting at $25,000 for single returns and $40,000 for joint returns, and 16 percent starting at $37,500 and $65,000 for single and joint returns, respectively. The maximum combined marginal rate in all cases would be 30 percent.

4. B-G computes the regular tax on the basis of the adjusted gross income less deductions and exemptions, while surtaxes are computed without applying any deductions and exemptions. In addition to these major changes in the current tax law, the B-G proposal would repeal the indexing of the marginal tax rates for general price inflation that is scheduled to become effective in 1985.

5. All realized capital gains are taxed as ordinary income, and the exemption of interest on newly issued revenue bonds is repealed.

Although the base broadening in the B-G bill appears to be well justified, it may not have gone far enough. This is especially true for the excluded items (for example, interest on tax-exempt general obligation municipal bonds) because they are excluded from both the regular tax and the surtax, while deducted items (such as interest on home mortgages) are excluded from the regular tax but not from the surtax. Given the political pressures to retain the preferred tax treatment of certain items of income and expenditures, the B-G proposal may go as far as is politically feasible.

It would be highly desirable to broaden the B-G bill to include appropriate taxation of unrealized capital gains and social security benefits. In the case of the B-G proposal it would be desirable to retain the limited indexing of the current law. The K-K proposal retains this feature. On the other hand K-K, unlike B-G, postpones for ten years the full taxation of realized capital gains as ordinary income, a proposal that seems undesirable. Also it would be desirable to extend indexing to the taxation of income from capital, both in the form of capital gains and interest, so that general price inflation would not affect the tax liabilities of income from capital. Further consideration might be given to the taxation of charitable contributions in the K-K bill and, perhaps, to the taxation of interest from newly issued general state and local government obligations in both the B-G and K-K bills.

Almost any major change in the tax laws will have important and sometimes serious one-time or transitional effects on some taxpayers, and this is true of the B-G proposal. Home owners would be adversely affected by an increase in the after-tax cost of owning a home and by a decline in its market value. The K-K proposal would also adversely affect home owners but probably by not as much as the B-G proposal. Similarly stock prices may be adversely affected, at least to a moderate extent, by a reduction in the tax advantage associated with realized capital gains.

Although it might be possible to minimize these and other transitional problems through a gradual phase-in of the new provisions or through grandfather clauses, initially major losses of tax revenues would result. To undo these effects, complex further changes would be required in these proposals both to ensure that the deficit is not raised further and to maintain reduced marginal rates for all taxpayers without increasing the relative tax burden for the lower-income groups. If these complications are to be avoided, the political process would have to accept the fact that some groups will be harmed.

To realize the goals of the B-G proposal or the K-K proposal, it is important that as a minimum the base-broadening measures already incorporated into these proposals be adopted as a whole. If some of these measures are omitted for political reasons or greatly modified because of transitional problems, the resulting tax system may increase the already swollen government deficit, change the tax incidence as planned under the proposal, quite possibly in a regressive direction, and might perpetuate economic inefficiency. From an economic viewpoint it would be preferable to expand rather than to contract the base-broadening measures.

If it becomes impossible to adopt the B-G, the K-K, or some similar proposal without substantial dilution of its provisions, an entirely different alternative should be considered. One alternative would be to strengthen the minimum tax gradually from the current 20 percent to a somewhat higher level, such as the upper level of 30 percent in B-G. Such a step would improve the equity of the current tax system and contribute somewhat to increasing the federal revenue. As the tax rate is increased, the base of the minimum tax could then be made more and more complete and made applicable to progressively lower-income classes. This would further increase total tax revenues and allow reduction of marginal rates, together with some increases in personal exemptions.

Such an approach would help to minimize the risk of substantial distributional and economic consequences of any major change in the tax law, as well as the severity of any transitional difficulties. It might also help to reduce the political resistance to the needed changes in the income tax system, including the highly desirable broadening of the tax base.

Corporate Income Tax Reform

The burden of corporate taxes is ultimately borne by individuals: consumers, labor, corporate stockholders, and other investors. Yet there is a separate corporate tax. The major justification usually given for such a separate tax is that the corporation is considered an independent entity and granted limited liability, permitting the accumulation of undistributed and untaxed wealth and the amassing of economic power. A second justification is that the corporate tax is a convenient mechanism for collecting a large amount of government revenue.

The major criticism of a separate system of corporate taxation has been the double taxation at both the corporate and individual levels of capital income generated by corporations, placing an undue burden on corporate investment with a consequent loss in economic efficiency. Other important criticisms are that under the present system, the effective corporate tax rates are not related to the circumstances of the individual beneficial owners of the corporate stock, contributing to inequities in the burden of taxation, and that the present form of corporate taxation encourages retention of corporate earnings and debt financing at the expense of external equity financing.

Most of these objections could be overcome with some form of integration of the corporate and individual income taxes, either making the corporate tax a withholding tax for individuals or completely abolishing corporate income taxation. It would also be desirable to eliminate the extremely large disparities in corporate tax rates on different investments, to reduce to the extent possible the discrepancies between corporate taxable and economic income, and to minimize the asymmetric treatment of corporate gains and losses under current law.

The ultimate improvement of the present system of corporate taxation may require the full integration of corporate and personal income taxes in which stockholders pay directly or indirectly the equivalent of the corporate tax on their pro-rata shares of retained earnings as well as dividends. Without such full integration there could be a substantial loss of corporate tax revenues (amounting to over $60 billion in 1983), which would have to be made up in some other form. In addition the cancellation of the present value of deferred taxes and subsequent taxes on future profits from existing corporate investment, estimated to be $427 billion in 1981, would provide an extremely large windfall profit to stockholders.

The main proposals for immediate reform of the current system of corporate income taxes considered in this study are those contained in the B-G bill. Similar provisions are contained in other flat tax proposals. The major provisions of the B-G proposal for corporate taxes are the imposition of a uniform tax rate of 30 percent for all corporations, the repeal of most current tax deductions, credits, and exclusions that distort investment decisions, and a new depreciation system that attempts to ensure the equivalence of book and economic depreciation. The decrease in tax revenues attributable to the reduction in the basic corporate tax rate would be approximately offset by the increase in revenue resulting from the elimination of investment tax credits, accelerated depreciation allowances, and a large number of other existing tax deductions.

The major improvement in corporate taxation under B-G and similar proposals would be the elimination of the unequal tax treatment of different corporations and investment activities, which should result in improved equity and allocational efficiency. For reasons discussed in the study, the elimination of special investment tax incentives should not have the substantial adverse effect on investment in the long run feared by some economists. Also the study concludes that most other deficiencies in the current system of corporate taxes seem to be attenuated (though not eliminated) by the proposed B-G changes, largely as a result of the marked decrease in the basic corporate and individual tax rates and the general reduction in rate differentials.

Since B-G grandfathers tax expenditure items applicable to capital outlays made prior to the enactment of the proposed legislation, the one-time capital losses involved for individual corporations that are adversely affected generally should not be large. Estimates made by the Joint Committee on Taxation suggest that the B-G elimination of tax preferences on new investment and the associated reduction in the statutory corporate tax rates approximately offset each other for the next few years. Since the reduction in statutory corporate tax rates by about one-third would persist after the tax preference on old investments had been charged off, the enactment of B-G would still entail a moderate cancellation in the implicit present value of the future taxes on existing investment even at the present high level of interest rates, resulting in a significant capital gain for corporations as a whole in the transitional process. (There would be significantly larger capital gains associated with the K-K flat tax proposal for corporations since accelerated depreciation would be retained.) As a consequence most corporations would benefit, though others would be hurt in the transition.

It is not clear whether the gains or losses to individual corporations would be sufficiently large to warrant remedial action through either a system of transitional credits and surtaxes or a phasing-in period, but we believe that in the absence of demonstrated extreme hardship, the changes in corporate taxation proposed by B-G might legitimately be considered as constituting normal business risk.

The study spells out a number of further improvements that could be made in the B-G proposed changes in corporate taxes. It also points out that their proposal, with or without these changes, and other flat tax proposals represent an improvement over current tax law. The ultimate improvement would entail full integration of corporate and personal income taxes. This could be accomplished by one of two approaches. The first would entail the gradual reduction of corporate taxes from the B-G 30 percent until they can be set at zero, offsetting the reduction by the inclusion of a pro-rata share of corporate retained earnings in the stockholders' personal tax base. Another approach would also gradually eliminate the double taxation of corporate income but retain corporate taxation as a convenient withholding device.

In achieving this objective of full integration, it will be necessary to ensure that total revenues to the government are not reduced, that regressivity is not introduced into the overall tax structure, and that stockholders are not provided with major windfall gains. The problems would be greatly reduced by the inclusion of corporate retained earnings in the stockholders' tax bases as full integration is achieved. Additional study is needed to determine whether further steps are required, such as temporary surtaxes on corporate income or prolonged phase-in periods. The enactment of the B-G proposal, which may be regarded as a first step toward integration of corporate and personal income taxes, would shed substantial light on the transitional costs likely to be involved in the subsequent move to full integration.

A final system of corporate taxation considered in the study is a corporate cash-flow tax, which has been proposed recently as a substitute for the corporate income tax. The study briefly examines the alleged merits of such taxation and finds no clear evidence of its improvement over income taxes, even abstracting from the formidable transitional problems it poses. The case for a cash-flow corporate tax would be stronger if the present system of personal income taxes were transformed to a consumption or expenditure basis.

New Consumption Taxes

In recent years some legislators and economists have proposed various forms of a consumption tax as either a substitute for or supplement to the current U.S. tax system, which for the most part is based on income. There are two basic forms of a consumption tax: a cash-flow tax and some type of sales tax or VAT. The study examines in detail the mechanics and variants of these taxes.

The arguments in favor of consumption taxes are that such taxes would simplify the tax structure, enhance equity, improve the allocation of investments, and encourage savings and investment. A consumption tax, at least in certain forms, is neutral with respect to the timing of consumption, whereas a tax on income favors current consumption over future consumption. More pragmatically the powerful interest groups now fighting tax reform may find a consumption tax less objectionable.

Some of the opposing arguments pertain to any form of a consumption tax, and some pertain to only specific forms of a consumption tax. The arguments opposing consumption taxes in general are that consumption taxes may lead to an undesirable concentration of wealth with the attendant economic power, might adversely affect the supply of labor, are less stabilizing in terms of the business cycle than income taxes, may alter the distribution of the tax burden in a regressive way, and would entail substantial transitional problems.

One of the most serious transitional problems is that

those who had saved some of their taxable income to use for consumption in later life would be taxed twice: once when they earned the income and once when they consumed their savings. Thus the older generation would be taxed more heavily than the younger generation, who have not yet accumulated much savings.

Consumption taxes may lead to a greater concentration of wealth than income taxes. The seriousness of this tendency would hinge on the effect of a consumption tax on saving rates. Nonetheless, just as with income taxes and perhaps even more so here, any major reform of the tax system should be fully integrated with an effective inheritance tax.

A criticism specific to a VAT is that the tax would lead to an immediate increase in the cost-of-living indexes as currently calculated. Such increases would trigger cost-of-living clauses and might result in further demands for increased wages. The study examines ways to minimize this transitional problem.

Another criticism of the VAT is that, as it is administered in Europe, the calculation of the VAT is extremely cumbersome and would require substantial and costly changes in the accounting systems of most U.S. companies. However, there are other ways to calculate the VAT that utilize for the most part accounting numbers that U.S. companies already maintain as part of their accounting systems, and, if this is done correctly, it may be possible to cut down substantially on additional compliance costs. The study examines these other ways.

Whether a consumption tax is regressive depends on the specific type and magnitude of the tax. A cash-flow tax can be made as progressive as one pleases with an appropriate structure of marginal rates; however, a progressive cash-flow tax destroys the neutrality of a consumption tax as between current and future consumption. Thus a cash-flow tax cannot simultaneously be consistent with both the principle of tax neutrality as between future and current consumption and the principle of ability to pay. Yet a progressive cash-flow tax would still be more neutral as to how savings are invested than the current U.S. system.

As demonstrated in Europe, a VAT can be roughly consistent with both the principle of neutrality between future and current consumption and the principle of ability to pay. European countries have successfully obtained the desired degree of progressivity in their tax structures through a system of benefit payments, family allowances, and differential VATs according to the perceived necessity of the good; however, the taxing of goods at differential rates creates many administrative difficulties and, at the more fundamental level, distorts the types of consumption goods consumed.

To avoid the complications and distortions associated with multiple rates for the VAT, the study explores the feasibility of combining a flat VAT with a more progressive income tax than the current one or a progressive cash-flow tax levied directly on households. For the same level of total revenue, it should be noted that even though the marginal tax rates on income or cash flow would have to be more progressive than under an income tax, the total direct tax paid by households in any income class could be less than it is today, with an indirect tax (the VAT) making up that difference. Moreover with appropriate benefit payments and family allowances, it may be possible to exempt a large number of households from having to file any tax form at all.

After the transitional problems are resolved, a consumption-based tax can conceptually result in a less complicated tax system since it is unnecessary to allocate cash expenditures for capital equipment made in one tax period as expenses to other tax periods. Thus there would be no need for the extensive regulations on depreciation present in the current code. And there would be no need to allocate cash income received in one tax period for services to be rendered in subsequent tax periods to those tax periods.

The study points out, however, that the specific proposals for progressive cash-flow taxes may lead to major tax abuses since it is easier under a cash-flow concept than under an income concept to shift the tax base from one tax period to another. Moreover a cash-flow tax would be considerably more complicated to implement than an income tax at the individual level. It should be noted that no country has yet successfully introduced a cash-flow tax into its tax system. The possibility of tax evasion under a VAT is undoubtedly less than under a cash-flow tax and may be less than under the current U.S. tax system.

The argument that the replacement of an income tax by a consumption tax would lead to increased savings is problematical. Whether such taxes would encourage additional savings largely hinges on the relationship of overall savings to after-tax rates of return. There does not appear to be a strong empirical relationship between savings and after-tax rates of return, so it is doubtful that a consumption tax would greatly stimulate savings.

The study points out that it would be possible to attain some, though not all, of the advantages of a consumption tax with fewer transitional costs and risks by expanding the use of IRAs. It notes, however, that expanding the role of IRAs moves the tax system in the opposite direction from that espoused by those who wish to broaden the tax base and probably would require more progressivity in other parts of the tax system to maintain the current distribution of the tax burden by income class. Moreover providing a tax incentive for IRAs may encourage households merely to shift their existing assets and savings to IRAs with no effect on the overall saving rate. Yet once funds were in IRAs, particularly in self-directed IRAs, the tax system would be more neutral than it is today as to how such funds are invested, one of the advantages of consumption-type taxes.

2

The Current U.S. Tax Structure and Its Incidence

Overview of the Tax System

From 1955 through 1959 the total receipts of federal, state, and local governments averaged 25.8 percent of GNP (gross national product). This percentage gradually increased through the 1960s, was relatively constant through the 1970s, averaging 31.0 percent, and then increased again to 31.9 percent by 1982. In 1983 this percentage declined to 31.0 percent, roughly the same as the average percentage in the 1970s (table 2.1).

From 1955 through the end of the 1960s, both federal and state and local governments saw an increase in their receipts as a percentage of GNP. From 1970 on, the receipts of state and local governments as a percentage of GNP showed no clear trend, fluctuating around 11.6 percent. In the 1970s the receipts of the federal government fluctuated around 19.2 percent and then increased gradually to 20.7 percent in 1981.[1] In 1983 federal receipts declined to 19.0 percent, slightly less than the average in the 1970s.

From 1955 on, state and local governments collected an increasing share of all government receipts. In the years 1955 through 1959 state and local receipts represented 29.8 percent of all governmental receipts. In 1983 this percentage was 38.7 percent.

Table 2.1
Receipts of federal, state, and local governments as a percentage of
GNP

Years[a]	Total[b]	Federal[b]	State and local[b]
1955–1959	25.8	18.1	7.7
1960–1964	27.5	18.5	9.0
1965–1969	28.9	19.1	9.9
1970–1974	31.0	19.2	11.6
1975–1979	31.0	19.3	11.7
1980	31.4	20.1	11.3
1981	31.9	20.7	11.2
1982	31.1	19.6	11.6
1983	31.0	19.0	12.0

Source: *Economic Report of the President* (February 1984), tables B-1, B-75, B-76.
Note: All taxes are on a cash basis except for corporations, which are on an accrual basis.
a. When range of years is shown, percentage figures are averages of the individual years.
b. Federal Reserve profits are deducted from federal and total tax receipts in calculating receipts as a percentage of GNP.
c. Federal grants-in-aid are excluded.

Sources of Revenue

In 1982, the last year for which detailed national income accounts were available at the time of this writing, the individual income tax provided approximately half of all federal receipts, and payroll taxes accounted for about a third (table 2.2). In total, 85.2 percent of all federal receipts were from individual income taxes and payroll taxes. The balance of federal receipts came from corporate taxes, excise taxes, estate and gift taxes, and other miscellaneous taxes.

The two main sources of state and local receipts are sales taxes and property taxes, together representing 56.2 percent of their receipts. Individual income taxes are the third most important source of state and local receipts, repre-

Table 2.2
Federal, state, and local taxes and other revenues, by major source, 1982

Major source	Revenues[a]	
	Amounts (billions)	Percentage of total
Federal		
Individual income	$296.7	50.4
Corporation income[b]	31.1	5.3
Excises	32.4	5.5
Estates and gift	7.6	1.3
Payroll	204.5	34.7
Other	16.2	2.8
Total	588.5	100.0
State and local		
Individual income	51.8	16.0
Corporation income[b]	12.7	3.9
Sales	95.5	29.5
Estate and gift	2.6	0.8
Payroll	4.0	1.2
Property	86.5	26.7
Other	71.0	21.9
Total	324.1	100.0
All levels		
Individual income	348.5	38.2
Corporation income	43.8	4.8
Sales and excises	127.9	14.0
Estate and gift	10.2	1.1
Payroll	208.4	22.8
Property	86.5	9.5
Other	87.3	9.6
Total	912.6	100.0

Sources: *Survey of Current Business* 63 (July 1983): tables 3.2, 3.3, 3.4, 3.6; *Economic Report of the President* (February 1984), table B-83.
a. Revenues are defined as receipts in the national income accounts less contributions for social insurance other than payroll taxes. Federal grants-in-aid are not included in state and local receipts.
b. Federal Reserve profits are deducted from corporate income tax receipts at the federal and total levels.

senting 16.0 percent of the receipts.[2] The other categories of state and local receipts represent a wide range of taxes and fees, ranging from motor vehicle licenses and fines to education and health charges. Payroll and corporate income taxes are not important sources of state and local receipts. (These are aggregate figures for all states and localities. In any specific state or locality the relative importance of these taxes could be quite different from the aggregate.)

For all levels of government combined, individual income taxes and payroll taxes provide 61.0 percent of receipts. The corporate income tax is not currently a major source of governmental receipts, representing only 4.8 percent of receipts.[3] Sales and excise taxes together account for 14.0 percent of total receipts. Roughly a quarter of these taxes are federal excise taxes, almost half representing the windfall profit tax and a quarter liquor and tobacco taxes.

In sum, the current collection of taxes and other receipts is heavily weighted toward individual income and payroll taxes. Sales and excise taxes are the next most important sources of revenues, but these revenues are only about a quarter of the revenues collected through individual income and payroll taxes.

Trends in Sources of Receipts

Joseph Pechman has prepared some estimates of the impact of the recent changes in the tax law on the level and types of taxes to be collected in 1985.[4] These estimates are based on a somewhat broader definition of income and slightly different definitions of taxes and receipts. They thus differ from the estimates based on the national income accounts. Since Pechman used the same definitions to produce figures for 1966, 1975, and 1980 and forecasts for 1985, his numbers can be used to evaluate overall trends. They should not be used in comparison with national income figures.

As a source of receipts for all government units, individual income taxes and payroll taxes will be a more important source of receipts in 1985 than in 1980 or 1975 (table 2.3). Corporate income taxes will represent an even smaller percentage of total receipts than they did in 1980. Sales and excise taxes will become less important in 1985 than in 1980, primarily due to a predicted leveling of the growth rates of these taxes at the state and local level. Payroll taxes will represent a greater proportion of receipts due to a rapid growth of these taxes at the federal level.

As a percentage of Pechman's income numbers, individual income taxes at the federal level will be about the same in 1985 as in 1980 but more than in 1975 (table 2.4). Payroll taxes will be a relatively more important source of revenue in 1985 than in 1980 or 1975. Corporate taxes will decline in importance at the federal level and be virtually unchanged at the state and local levels. Finally sales and excise taxes at the state and local levels will decline as a percentage of income. Federal taxes and receipts as a percentage of income will be less in 1985 than in 1980 but greater than those of 1975.

Tax Incidence

Problems of Measurement

Tax incidence means the effects that a particular tax or a collection of taxes has on the well-being of individuals in the economy. Since the impact of the total U.S. tax system is the primary focus of this study, it is tempting to pose a global question: Compared to the situation in which there is no tax, how much worse off are individuals of various classes under the existing or proposed tax system? The

Table 2.3
Percentage distribution of receipts and taxes by federal, state, and local, and total, 1975, 1980, 1985

Major source	1966	1975	1980	1985
Federal				
Individual income tax		47.3	49.2	50.9
Corporate income tax		14.5	14.2	9.1
Property tax		0.0	0.0	0.0
Sales and excise tax		6.1	3.8	3.4
Payroll tax		32.7	33.3	36.6
Personal property and motor vehicle		0.0	0.0	0.0
Total		100.0	100.0	100.0
State and local				
Individual income tax		16.1	20.3	26.3
Corporate income tax		4.6	5.1	5.3
Property tax		36.8	30.4	28.9
Sales and excise tax		39.1	41.8	36.8
Payroll tax		0.0	0.0	0.0
Personal property and motor vehicle		3.4	2.5	2.6
Total		100.0	100.0	100.0
All levels				
Individual income tax	33.7	36.5	40.5	43.0
Corporate income tax	17.0	11.1	11.5	8.4
Property tax	13.0	12.5	9.2	8.8
Sales and excise tax	19.3	17.5	15.3	13.5
Payroll tax	16.0	21.4	23.3	25.5
Personal property and motor vehicle	1.0	1.2	0.8	0.8
Total	100.0	100.0	100.0	100.0

question also appears to have an answer. Since we can in principle calculate, aside from the statistical difficulties, the resources available to the individual gross of tax (income in some sense) and the total amount of tax paid by him or her, one might say that the person is worse off due to the tax system precisely by the amount of taxes paid. The mea-

Table 2.4
Receipts and taxes as a percentage of Pechman's income estimates, by federal, state, and local, and total, 1975, 1980, 1985

Major source	1975	1980	1985
Federal			
Individual income tax	7.8	9.0	8.9
Corporate income tax	2.4	2.6	1.6
Property tax	0.0	0.0	0.0
Sales and excise tax	1.0	0.7	0.6
Payroll tax	5.4	6.1	6.4
Personal property and motor vehicle	0.0	0.0	0.0
Total	16.5	18.3	17.5
State and local			
Individual income tax	1.4	1.6	2.0
Corporate income tax	0.4	0.4	0.4
Property tax	3.2	2.4	2.2
Sales and excise tax	3.4	3.3	2.8
Payroll tax	0.0	0.0	0.0
Personal property and motor vehicle	0.3	0.2	0.2
Total	8.7	7.9	7.6
All levels			
Individual income tax	9.2	10.6	10.8
Corporate income tax	2.8	3.0	2.1
Property tax	3.2	2.4	2.2
Sales and excise tax	4.4	4.0	3.4
Payroll tax	5.4	6.1	6.4
Personal property and motor vehicle	0.3	0.2	0.2
Total	25.2	26.2	25.1

sure of the burden is the ratio of the amount of tax paid to the before-tax income.

This reasoning, unfortunately, is subject to a number of serious objections, which can be grouped into three categories.[5] First, it is difficult to imagine the economy with no taxes at all, since there is always need for some public goods and therefore there will always be some government expenditures.

Second, this argument assumes that nothing else

changes when a very large tax system is imposed or removed; in particular income before tax would remain the same for all individuals with or without the tax system. This is a clearly unreasonable argument. When such a large change is imposed on the economy, there is little reason to believe that relative prices of goods and services would remain the same or that the distribution of income before tax can be the same. Suppose that an individual receives an income of $20,000 if there were no tax and an income before tax of $22,000 when there is a tax. If the applicable tax rate (including all forms of taxes) is, say, 20 percent, the income after tax would be 80 percent of $22,000, or $17,600. In order to measure the total effect of the tax system on this individual, we should be comparing $20,000 with $17,600, not $22,000 with $17,600.[6] The latter comparison may or may not have any close relationship with the former comparison; yet since we do not know the income that would occur absent all taxes and have very little hope of ever estimating it, the only comparison that can be made from data realistically is the latter comparison.

Third, there is the difficulty of defining groups that are meaningful and determining exactly who belongs to each of the groups. For example, when we speak of the bottom decile of the size distribution of income, statistically the measure of income used is usually one calendar year. Upon reflection, however, it becomes apparent that such a measure of income is probably inappropriate if we are considering effects of taxes on income distribution as we normally understand the phrase in policy discussions. Among low-income persons in any particular year classified by the statistical measure of income for that year, there are those whose income is very low because they are very young, those who are older and retired (though this is much less true now because of the increases in social security benefits), and those who have had a bad year for one rea-

son or another, as well as persons who are poor throughout their lives. The focus of much discussion of public
policy is this last group: those who are poor throughout
their lives. We may be interested in elderly persons and
young ones too, but many of them earn much higher income during the middle period of their lives. Yet statistically it is hard to distinguish among these groups, and, for
the lack of data, they are normally not treated separately in
the analysis of tax incidence.

To make our analysis less subject to these objections, we
must interpret our quantitative estimates modestly. We
cannot interpret these results as representing the total effects of the tax system compared to the taxless regime. The
reference position from which to compare the current tax
system or proposed revisions must be fairly close to the
current status of the economy, so that most conditions in
the economy, especially relative prices, can be expected to
remain approximately the same for the two situations. At
the same time the reference position must also have a simple, easily understood interpretation so that the comparison between it and the current condition has well-defined
significance.

The basis for comparison we use is the one in which the
real government expenditure is the same as the actual situation in question, and the tax system is a strictly proportional income tax with the rate sufficient to yield the
amount of revenue needed to keep the deficit in the government budget the same. Such a tax system is relatively
easy to interpret, and it is not so radically different from
the current condition as to make the comparison impossible because under the current tax system the ratio of tax
burden to a measure of income does not vary a great deal
among income classes. This is the notion of differential tax
incidence proposed by Richard Musgrave some years ago.[7]

Even in this more modest interpretation of quantitative

analysis, we should also keep in mind that what is measured is not the direct effect of tax change alone but the complex total effects, including the direct effects of taxes, as well as indirect effects due to changes in behavior of all persons and organizations in the economy in response to changes in taxes.

Finally, in view of the third point raised, when we observe that, for instance, the tax burden of a particular group is 2 percent higher under the current system than it would have been in the reference situation, we are not necessarily comparing the same group of individuals. Under two different tax systems the membership in the particular group may be quite different, and hence we cannot say that a specific individual is given a 2 percent heavier burden in one situation than in another. All we can say is that a specific group, with possibly different memberships in two different conditions, bears different tax burdens under two different tax systems and that the tax distribution in one situation favors or disfavors a particular income class more than that in the second situation.

In applying the incidence analysis to actual economic data, especially when considering the whole tax structure, it is necessary to make assumptions on whom the direct effect of any specific tax falls. For example, it is generally assumed that federal personal income tax reduces the income of income earners by the full amount of the tax.[8] In the case of sales tax or excise tax it is assumed that the taxes are paid by consumers in the form of higher price gross of taxes, not by sellers in the form of lower price net of taxes. On every tax that exists in the economy, we must make specific assumptions of this sort in order to obtain numerical estimates of the incidence of the tax system. Many of these assumptions are fairly reasonable, and others are not so reasonable, but the tax for which the assumption is made may be quite small and thus our overall conclusions may not depend on them significantly.[9]

The largest problem arises in the case of the corporate profit tax. Depending on a number of conditions, including the elasticity of demand for output of the corporation and elasticities of factor supplies, the corporate profit tax may raise prices of output and thus be borne by final purchasers of the output, or it may be borne by suppliers of factors in the form of lower compensations for their services. Depending on the factor elasticities and assumed behavior of the management, the tax burden may be split among labor, lenders of debt capital (bondholders), lenders of equity capital (stock owners), and consumers, or it can be borne by one or more of these groups. The assumption is often made that it is borne entirely by stock owners because the interest charges and the wage bill are deductible for tax purposes, but this is not entirely justified if the corporate management is able to maintain a lower wage rate or lower rate of interest on bonds in the presence of the tax relative to those maintainable when the tax is not present. Currently most economists are probably inclined to impute the corporate profit taxes to stock owners, but the justification for this assumption is not completely satisfactory.

Under the circumstances, in the numerical analysis reported in the next section, two alternative ways of imputing the corporate profit tax and making other necessary imputations are presented. In one case the computations are carried out in such a way that the resulting tax burden is most progressive relative to the income distribution. In the second the estimated tax burden is least progressive. We believe that the true answer lies between these two extremes but that it is probably closer to the most progressive case than to the least progressive case.

Impact of Taxes on Different Income Groups

Joseph Pechman and Benjamin Okner have prepared careful studies of the impact of all types of taxes on U.S. individuals in different income groups. Such estimates for 1966
and 1970 have been published.[10] Those for 1975, 1980, and
1985 have been made available to us by Dr. Pechman. (The
estimates for 1985 are based on current tax laws.[11]) All
show effective tax rates applicable to different income
groups, for federal and state and local taxes, both combined and separately for each of the major types of taxes:
taxes on individual and corporate incomes, real and personal property, sales, excises, and payrolls.

In these estimates the different types of taxes are combined to obtain composite effective tax rates by income
group. This obviously necessitates a difficult allocation of
taxes other than those on individual incomes to the appropriate income group, a process that requires controversial
assumptions about the impact on income of these other
taxes. Pechman and Okner have made eight sets of estimates of the composite effective tax rates by income class,
embodying what they regard as the most reasonable incidence assumptions.[12] We present here only two of these
sets of estimates, one based on the most progressive incidence assumptions and the other based on the least progressive assumptions.

In an attempt to approximate more closely an economist's definition of income for a household or family, Pechman and Okner use a concept of income for estimating the
burden of taxation that differs from the concept of adjusted
gross income used by the U.S. Department of the Treasury
Internal Revenue Service. Pechman and Okner derive family income from national income (composed of employees'
compensation, proprietor's income, net interest, net rental
income of individuals, and corporate profits before taxes)

Table 2.5
Effective rates of combined federal, state, and local taxes under two
sets of incidence assumptions, by adjusted family income class, 1985

	Incidence assumptions	
Adjusted family income	Most progressive	Least progressive
$0–5,000	46.9%	76.5%
$5,000–10,000	22.7	29.9
$10,000–15,000	21.4	25.6
$15,000–20,000	21.4	24.7
$20,000–25,000	22.0	24.8
$25,000–30,000	23.0	25.5
$30,000–50,000	23.7	25.5
$50,000–100,000	25.1	26.0
$100,000–500,000	25.1	22.9
$500,000–1 million	25.5	20.1
$1 million and over	27.1	18.2
All classes[a]	24.5	25.3

Source: Data provided by Joseph Pechman and based on MERGE file.
Note: Based on tax laws enacted prior to 1984.
a. Includes negative incomes not shown separately.

by adding transfer payments to individuals and accrued
capital gains (normalized) and then deducting income not
received by individuals and imputed interest.[13]

The effective rates of federal, state, and local taxes combined estimated for the year 1985 under current tax laws
are presented in table 2.5 for a wide range of absolute
incomes, under both the least and most progressive incidence assumptions. These two tax assumptions differ
mainly in the allocation of corporate income taxes between
stockholders and consumers and of employer-paid payroll
taxes between employees and consumers. The most progressive incidence assumptions point to some progression
in composite effective tax rates ranging from 22.7 percent
in the $5,000–10,000 income group[14] to 27.1 percent for
income of $1 million and over, with an average of 24.5
percent. The least progressive incidence assumptions

point to some regressivity in the composite tax structure, with a somewhat lower ratio of taxes to income for the top than for the lower income groups. The six other incidence assumptions provide results intermediate between the two sets of estimates we present; however, they are somewhat closer on average to the most progressive than to the least progressive estimates, suggesting at least a modest progressivity in the composite tax structure.

As would be expected, the estimated progressivity in the composite tax structure is mainly attributable to individual income taxes (table 2.6). Sales and excise taxes and payroll taxes are strongly regressive, while the incidence of corporate income taxes and property taxes on different income levels is critically dependent on the incidence assumptions made. Federal taxes as a whole are somewhat more progressive than state and local taxes. At the federal level the progressivity of the income tax slightly outweighs the regressivity of payroll taxes, leading to a very modest progressivity. At the state and local level the taxes are regressive on balance. But even the federal taxes are not progressive if the least progressive tax incidence assumptions are made (table 2.7).

It is of substantial interest to determine the trends in the effective tax rates paid by different income groups as a result of changes in taxes over the years 1966 through 1985 for which such data are available. In view of the noncomparability of absolute income levels over a period characterized by marked inflationary pressures and other significant cyclical and secular changes, the historical estimates in table 2.8 are presented in selected percentile form to provide such comparability. The data show a significant decline from 1966 to 1985 in the effective tax rates for the top percentile group but a more moderate decline for the top decile as a whole. Most of the declines for these two groups occurred between 1970 and 1975, with a more modest decline characterizing the 1980–1985 period. For the top percentile group the decline from 1966 to 1985 was 13.7 percent under the most progressive incidence assumptions and 7.4 percent under the least progressive assumptions. This decline in the overall burden of taxes for the top income class reflects mainly a decline in the effective rates of capital gains and corporate income taxes, an increase in payroll taxes falling mainly on the lower-income groups, and, subsequent to 1980, a lower ceiling on the maximum income tax.[15] In the top percentile group, it should be noted, a substantial proportion of family income as measured by Pechman and Okner reflects capital gains.

The progressivity in taxes for 1985 indicated by table 2.8 is not much different from that suggested by table 2.5, even though table 2.5 breaks out the very rich from the rest of the top percentile income group. This result is quite different from that obtained for prior years when the effective tax rate for the very rich was substantially higher than for the rest of the top percentile group. For the top percentile group as a whole the effective tax rate of 25.5 percent under the most progressive incidence assumption is 3.6 percent (percentage points) higher than the 21.9 percent figure for the bottom decile and 4.2 percent higher than the 21.3 percent figure for the second decile.[16] The relatively high figure for the bottom decile may be misleading in view of the large number of families with an annual income well below its normal level. Under the least progressive incidence assumptions the effective tax rate is estimated to be 4.4 percent lower for the top percentile group than for the second decile. Assuming that the correct incidence of taxes is somewhere between the two sets of figures but closer to those estimated under the most progressive incidence assumptions, there is still some progressivity in the tax structure, although it is likely to be rather modest.

There are three respects in which these estimates of the

Table 2.6
Effective rates of combined federal, state, and local taxes, by type of tax, under two sets of incidence assumptions, by adjusted family income class, 1985

Family income decile	Individual income tax	Corporation income tax	Property tax	Sales and excise taxes	Payroll taxes	Personal property and motor vehicle taxes	Total taxes
Most progressive tax assumptions							
First[a]	4.2%	0.5%	0.7%	7.0%	9.4%	0.1%	21.9%
Second	5.5	0.5	0.7	5.9	8.7	0.1	21.3
Third	6.9	0.6	0.9	5.0	8.0	0.1	21.4
Fourth	8.2	0.6	0.9	4.6	7.9	0.2	22.5
Fifth	9.1	0.7	1.0	4.3	7.8	0.2	23.1
Sixth	9.8	0.8	1.2	4.1	7.5	0.2	23.5
Seventh	10.3	0.8	1.3	3.9	7.2	0.2	23.7
Eighth	11.4	0.9	1.3	3.7	7.0	0.2	24.6
Ninth	12.2	1.2	1.7	3.3	6.4	0.2	25.1
Tenth[b]	12.6	2.5	2.7	2.4	4.9	0.2	25.2
Top 1 percent	12.8	5.7	4.4	1.1	1.4	0.1	25.5
All	10.9	1.8	2.0	3.4	6.2	0.2	24.5

Least progressive tax assumptions

First[a]	4.1	2.8	3.3	7.2	10.8	0.1	28.2
Second	5.4	2.3	2.5	5.7	9.5	0.1	25.6
Third	6.8	2.0	2.1	4.9	8.6	0.1	24.6
Fourth	8.1	1.9	2.1	4.6	8.4	0.2	25.2
Fifth	8.9	1.9	2.1	4.2	8.1	0.2	25.3
Sixth	9.6	1.9	2.1	4.0	7.8	0.2	25.6
Seventh	10.0	1.9	2.1	3.8	7.4	0.2	25.4
Eighth	11.2	1.8	2.2	3.7	7.2	0.2	26.3
Ninth	12.0	1.9	2.3	3.2	6.5	0.2	26.1
Tenth[b]	12.6	2.1	2.3	2.4	5.0	0.2	24.5
Top 1 percent	13.4	2.6	2.2	1.1	1.8	0.1	21.2
All	10.9	2.1	2.3	3.4	6.5	0.2	25.3

Source: See table 2.5.
a. Includes only units in the sixth to tenth percentiles.
b. Excludes top percentile.

Table 2.7
Effective rates of federal and state-local taxes separately, using two sets of assumptions about tax incidence, by adjusted family income class, 1985

Family income decile	Most progressive tax assumptions			Least progressive tax assumptions		
	Federal	State-local	Total	Federal	State-local	Total
First[a]	13.9%	8.0%	21.9%	16.9%	11.3%	28.2%
Second	14.5	6.8	21.3	16.7	8.9	25.6
Third	15.0	6.5	21.4	16.7	7.9	24.6
Fourth	16.0	6.5	22.5	17.4	7.8	25.2
Fifth	16.7	6.4	23.1	17.7	7.6	25.3
Sixth	16.9	6.6	23.5	17.9	7.7	25.6
Seventh	17.0	6.7	23.7	17.8	7.7	25.5
Eighth	17.8	6.9	24.6	18.5	7.8	26.3
Ninth	18.0	7.1	25.1	18.4	7.7	26.1
Tenth[b]	17.5	7.6	25.2	17.3	7.2	24.5
Top 1 percent	16.5	9.0	25.5	14.9	6.3	21.2
All	17.2	7.3	24.5	17.7	7.6	25.3

Source: See table 2.5.
a. Includes only units in the sixth to tenth percentiles.
b. Excludes top percentile.

tax incidence in the different income groups understate the progressivity effected by government fiscal policy.[17] First, although social welfare tax payments are included in the composite effective tax rates presented in table 2.8, these estimates do not net out social welfare benefits or transfer payments to the different groups. In view of the incidence of tax payments and benefits among different income groups, the use in these tables of gross instead of net figures associated with social welfare programs tends to understate the progressivity of fiscal policy. Although detailed relevant data have not been published, Pechman has provided estimates for 1985.[18] Based on these data, table 2.9 shows the effective rates of taxation net of social welfare transfer payments by adjusted family income class (less transfers) and, for comparative purposes, the effective rates of taxation gross of such transfer payments. Thus on this measure of fiscal burden, government fiscal policy is quite progressive in its incidence on different income groups until the $50,000–100,000 income level under the most progressive incidence assumptions and until the $30,000–50,000 income level under the least progressive assumptions. However, the progressivity of fiscal burden may be overstated by the estimates in table 2.9 in the perspective of lifetime rather than current annual income. The reason is that a high proportion of the families receiving social security benefits are classified in the lowest income classes because they are retired and would have substantially higher permanent income and net worth.

Table 2.9 does provide some limited insights into the fiscal burdens (positive or negative) borne by different income groups, where such burdens are defined as the difference between taxes paid and direct benefits received under social welfare programs. But it does not attempt to allocate government expenditures on all other programs (defense, education, roads, police, fire and disease prevention and

Table 2.8
Effective rates of combined federal, state, and local taxes under two
sets of incidence assumptions, by relative income ranking, 1966–1985

Decile income group	1966	1970	1975	1980	1985
Most progressive incidence assumptions					
First[a]	16.8%	18.8%	21.2%	20.6%	21.9%
Second	18.9	19.5	20.0	20.3	21.3
Third	21.7	20.8	20.5	20.6	21.4
Fourth	22.6	23.2	22.0	21.8	22.5
Fifth	22.8	24.0	23.0	22.5	23.1
Sixth	22.7	24.1	23.3	23.1	23.5
Seventh	22.7	24.3	23.6	23.8	23.7
Eighth	23.1	24.6	24.4	25.3	24.6
Ninth	23.3	25.0	25.3	26.0	25.1
Tenth[b]	30.1	30.7	27.1	27.4	25.2
Top 1 percent	39.2	39.0	28.5	27.6	25.5
All	25.2	26.1	25.0	25.2	24.5
Least progressive incidence assumptions					
First[a]	27.5	25.8	29.6	28.9	28.2
Second	24.8	24.2	24.2	25.7	25.6
Third	26.0	24.2	23.4	24.7	24.6
Fourth	25.9	25.9	24.6	25.4	25.2
Fifth	25.8	26.4	25.3	25.5	25.3
Sixth	25.6	26.3	25.3	25.7	25.6
Seventh	25.5	26.2	25.5	26.3	25.5
Eighth	25.5	26.4	26.0	27.6	26.3
Ninth	25.1	26.1	26.3	27.7	26.1
Tenth[b]	25.9	27.8	24.2	25.2	24.5
Top 1 percent	28.6	31.0	21.9	21.8	21.2
All	25.9	26.7	25.5	26.3	25.3

Source: See table 2.5.
a. Includes only units in the sixth to tenth percentiles.
b. Excludes top 1 percent.

Table 2.9
Effective rates of combined federal, state, and local tax rates versus rates of combined taxes less transfer payments under two sets of incidence assumptions, by adjusted family income class, 1985

| | Incidence assumptions | | | |
| | Most progressive | | Least progressive | |
Adjusted family income[a]	Combined tax rates	Less transfers	Combined tax rates	Less transfers
$0–5,000	43.9%	− 184.9%	83.3%	− 113.4%
$5,000–10,000	25.4	− 46.8	30.8	− 41.2
$10,000–15,000	24.9	− 14.4	28.7	− 10.9
$15,000–20,000	25.8	− 2.2	28.1	− 1.3
$20,000–25,000	26.1	5.6	28.6	8.1
$25,000–30,000	26.5	12.0	28.6	13.2
$30,000–50,000	26.9	18.9	28.8	20.7
$50,000–100,000	27.6	23.3	28.5	24.2
$100,000–500,000	26.1	23.6	23.9	21.6
$500,000–1 million	25.8	25.1	20.3	19.6
$1 million and over	27.2	26.9	18.3	18.1
All classes[b]	27.1	16.3	28.0	17.3

Source: See table 2.5.
Note: Based on tax laws enacted prior to 1984.
a. Less transfers, as opposed to Table 2.5, which uses adjusted family income inclusive of transfer income.
b. Includes negative incomes.

control, conservation, and so forth) to the presumed groups of beneficiaries. If our interest in fiscal burden estimates is to relate taxes paid by families in different income groups to their ability to pay, perhaps the most significant single set of measures is that relating to the gross tax burden (as in tables 2.5 to 2.8). If a broader measure of fiscal burden is desired, however, it can be obtained by netting out the benefits subsequently received under social welfare programs (as in table 2.9) or by omitting both taxes and benefits under such programs in the tax burden estimates, treating the insurance aspect of social welfare programs separately. An even broader measure of the fiscal burden may be appropriate if our concern is to determine whether families in different income groups pay more in total taxes than they receive in total direct and indirect benefits (and if so how much). For this purpose we would have to allocate all types of government expenditures to specific population groups, an almost impossible task for a high proportion of government outlays. The meaning and usefulness of the resulting comprehensive measure of fiscal burden, which essentially involves the distribution of the utility of public goods among these different groups, are open to question.

Some of the difficulties in estimating and interpreting such a comprehensive measure of fiscal burden are illustrated by the results of a recent attempt to estimate all net outlays or net receipts as a ratio of income for different economic groups.[19] Unfortunately not much confidence can be placed in these estimates, which show substantially negative net tax payments for the lower-income classes and substantially positive net payments for the upper classes and which probably greatly exaggerate the implied progressivity of the difference between total tax payments and total direct and implied benefits. Thus Ruggles and Higgins allocate expenditures on "police," "fire," and federal and state and local "unallocable" outlays (including defense) on the basis of population rather than income or net worth, a questionable treatment, especially for national defense. If federal "unallocable" outlays alone are allocated on the basis of income, the excess of taxes over benefits for the highest income decile is reduced from 23.5 percent to 12.9 percent of income. If allocated on the basis of net worth, taxes would no longer exceed benefits for this income class.[20] The allocation of police, fire, and state and local unallocable expenditures by family income, and even more so by net worth, might eliminate most or even all of the remaining progressivity. Clearly we do not have an adequate basis for approximating the progressiveness or regressiveness of the excess of taxes over all direct and indirect benefits for different economic groups.

A second respect in which the estimates presented in the tables in this chapter may understate the progressivity of taxes is that these estimates show the impact of taxation on the income actually received by the different income groups rather than the impact on before-tax income that would have been received in the absence of any taxes. One result of taxation is to induce taxpayers, especially those subject to high tax rates, to favor tax-sheltered investments such as municipal bonds that yield lower before-tax returns even though they have higher after-tax yields. It is difficult to impute the changes in before-tax incomes required to adjust for this effect of taxes on the before-tax return to capital; however, it would appear that the absence of such an adjustment leads to a greater understatement of tax effects on the upper- than on the lower-income groups, again resulting in an understatement of the progressivity of taxes. One estimate of the potential effect of such an adjustment suggests that it may be fairly substantial.[21]

The final respect in which the data presented in the tables on tax incidence may understate the progressivity of taxes relates to the effect of inflation on capital gains included in the Pechman-Okner estimates of income. These income estimates include all nominal capital gains on corporate stock and other assets rather than the change in current prices of the real capital gains.[22] Thus for corporate stock Pechman-Okner use book retained earnings as an estimate of normalized capital gains on corporate stock, though presumably if the market is rational, it would be more appropriate to use retained earnings adjusted for inflation distortions. This would reflect the difference between economic and book charges against assets, as well as the at least partially offsetting effect of inflation on the liabilities side.[23] Available data suggest that in inflationary periods corporate economic earnings are appreciably lower than book earnings, and therefore stock prices are adversely affected.[24] As a consequence, because corporate stock is predominantly held by the upper-income groups, the Pechman-Okner estimates would overstate the income and understate the effective tax rates paid by these groups in inflationary periods. The 1985 estimates would be affected in this manner but less than in 1975 or 1980 since they reflect a lower inflation rate and greater acceleration of depreciation charges.

In summary the available data on the relative tax burden by income class do not yield an unambiguous answer on the burden of the current overall tax structure; however, they do seem to point to some progressiveness in spite of the recent movements toward equality of tax rates among different income groups.[25] However, this modest remaining progressivity could easily be transformed into regressivity should there be any major uncompensated changes in the current tax structure aimed at reducing taxes on property income at the expense of labor income or converting taxes to a primarily consumption rather than income basis. On the other hand the fiscal burden defined as the difference between taxes paid and benefits or transfer payments received by different economic groups (as a percentage of family income) might remain progressive for the lower-income classes.

Although income is generally accepted as the best measure of taxpaying ability, relative tax burdens also could be analyzed by comparing taxes with family wealth or consumption. Unfortunately, satisfactory current data on taxes paid by wealth or consumption size groups are not available. It is known, however, that with unimportant exceptions, wealth rises appreciably more rapidly than income as income (or wealth) increases, while consumption rises appreciably less rapidly. As a result the current burden of taxes is likely to be strongly regressive by wealth group and strongly progressive by consumption group. Thus in 1962–1963 the ratio of nonhuman wealth or net worth to total wealth (human as well as nonhuman), which is a multiple of roughly one-tenth the net worth to income ratio, is estimated to have varied between 0.33 in the $10,000–100,000 net worth class and 0.85 in the over-$1 million class.[26] This would imply that if taxes were roughly proportional to income, the over-$1 million net worth group would have a ratio of taxes to net worth well under half that of the $10,000–100,000 net worth group, indicating marked regressiveness of current taxes on a wealth rather than income basis.

Further evidence that the burden of taxes is relatively lower on a wealth than on an income basis for the more affluent families is provided by a matching of estate tax returns filed in 1977 and income tax data for the years 1974 through 1980.[27] This analysis indicates that gross capital income as a percentage of wealth declined steadily from 12.4 percent in the under-$100,000 wealth group to 2.2 percent in the $2.5 million or more group. Part of this difference, of course, reflects the greater incentive for high-income taxpayers to favor tax-sheltered investments.

The most recent data available on the distribution of total U.S. family consumption by income groups (based on survey data for the period 1972–1973) provides a breakdown of total consumption by type of expenditure for a number of annual income groups below $25,000 and comparable information for all incomes above $25,000 treated as a single group.[28] The survey also collected data on family income, taxes, and savings or net changes in assets and liabilities, thus permitting the derivation of a second set of consumption estimates obtained as the difference between income after taxes and net changes in assets and liabilities. The published consumption estimates, which are based on the detailed expenditures data, point to total consumption for the average family generally in excess of income for annual incomes below $5,000, probably reflecting both measurement error and differences between income received that year and a more normal income level for the family. For the $5,000–6,000 income level the ratio of consumption to before-tax income was 98.5 percent, falling steadily to 45.9 percent for incomes over $25,000. Presumably these ratios would decline much further for substantially higher income levels. On an after-tax or disposable income basis the consumption-income ratio declines steadily from 96.8 percent in the $7,000–8,000 income class (the first group for which the survey shows consumption exceeding disposable income) to 56.8 percent in the over-$25,000 income group. All of these ratios would be increased somewhat by adjusting the survey data to national income totals, but the sharp downward trend in the relative importance of consumption as income rises is not affected appreciably.[29]

If consumption from these same data is estimated as the difference between disposable income and saving (net change in assets and liabilities including personal insurance, retirement and pension funds), however, the downward trend in the consumption-income ratio, though still substantial, is considerably reduced. From the available information it is not clear which of the two sets of total consumption estimates by income group is the more reliable, but survey estimates of total consumption and its composition for all income groups combined generally have been closer to the corresponding national income data than survey estimates of total savings and its composition.[30] As a result it is quite likely that a proportional tax on consumption would be highly regressive with respect to income, though the published consumption-income ratios presented previously probably overstate the degree to which this is true.

Impact of Taxes on Other Socioeconomic Groups and on Labor Income, Capital Income, and Consumption

Reasonably satisfactory and up-to-date data on the impact of taxes on population groups classified by socioeconomic characteristics other than income are not available. For 1966, however, Pechman and Okner present estimates of effective tax rates (under the most progressive and least progressive sets of assumptions) for families cross-classified by income decile and each of the following groupings: age of family head under 65 and over 65; home owners and renters; urban and rural-farm families; and single persons, married couples with no children, and married couples with two children.[31] In that year their estimates indicate that for all incomes combined, the composite effective tax rate paid by the 65-and-over group was not clearly different from that paid by the under-65 groups, with the comparative results depending on the tax incidence assumptions made. In the lower income classes the 65-and-over group appeared to pay somewhat lower effective tax rates, while for the upper incomes the 65-and-over group paid higher rates. The variations within income groups in the effective tax rates paid by age of head reflect differences in the sources of income, differences in applicable tax rates by age of head, and to a lesser extent special treatment of income received by the aged.

Unexpectedly, in view of the favorable income tax treatment of home owners, there was no consistent difference in 1966 between the effective composite tax rates paid by home owners and renters. Home owners paid higher effective tax rates than renters for the very lowest income groups but paid lower rates for the higher income groups. The surprisingly higher tax rates for home owners in the lowest income groups may reflect the fact that their normal income exceeded the income for the year to a greater extent than was true for renters.

As for the other socioeconomic groups urban families in 1966 generally paid slightly higher tax rates than rural-farm families for all income groups combined. The only sizable difference arose for the income groups at both ends of the income distribution. For the highest incomes the urban families paid higher tax rates, while for lowest incomes the reverse was true. These variations, when the year's income is held constant, probably reflect the differences in home ownership, in other property, and in normal income, as well as the favorable tax treatment of farm income.

In general, regardless of the incidence assumptions, the larger the size of the family, the smaller the tax paid in 1966 for most income groups. (A similar result would probably be true at the present time.) More surprisingly, however, an exception to this pattern was found in the lowest income deciles, where large families often paid higher taxes than smaller families, perhaps reflecting a relatively small tax value of the personal income tax exemptions and of income splitting for low incomes.

More up-to-date data on effective tax rates on sources and uses of income, provided by Joseph Pechman, show tax rates by population income decile on income from labor, income from capital, and consumption for the most progressive and least progressive sets of incidence assumptions (table 2.10). Under both sets of assumptions labor income is taxed more heavily than capital income for most income groups, and this is especially true under the least progressive assumptions. Under the most progressive incidence assumptions all types of income are taxed

Table 2.10
Effective rates of combined federal, state, and local taxes on sources and uses of income under two sets of incidence assumptions, by relative income ranking, 1985

Decile income group	Income from labor	Income from capital	Consumption taxes as a ratio of consumption	Consumption taxes as a ratio of income
Most progressive incidence assumptions				
First[a]	15.3%	26.8%	7.3%	7.1%
Second	17.5	19.3	7.4	6.6
Third	19.3	17.7	7.6	5.1
Fourth	20.4	16.6	7.8	4.8
Fifth	21.0	16.2	7.9	4.5
Sixth	21.3	15.6	8.0	4.3
Seventh	21.3	15.5	8.0	4.1
Eighth	21.5	15.7	7.9	4.0
Ninth	21.2	15.7	7.8	3.5
Tenth[b]	20.1	17.1	7.5	2.5
Top 1 percent	20.8	20.1	7.2	1.2
All	20.6	17.5	7.7	3.6
Least progressive incidence assumptions				
First[a]	12.4	20.1	16.5	16.5
Second	15.0	13.4	16.5	12.8
Third	17.0	12.3	16.4	10.8
Fourth	18.1	11.8	16.6	10.1
Fifth	18.9	11.5	16.9	9.3
Sixth	19.2	11.3	17.0	9.0
Seventh	19.3	10.9	17.1	8.6
Eighth	19.5	10.9	17.1	8.4
Ninth	19.3	10.4	17.2	7.6
Tenth[b]	18.2	10.2	17.4	5.8
Top 1 percent	19.9	11.0	17.4	2.9
All	18.6	10.8	17.0	7.8

Source: See table 2.5.
a. Includes only units in the sixth to tenth percentiles.
b. Excludes top 1 percent.

relatively more heavily than is consumption; however, under the least progressive incidence assumptions the differences in tax rates on income from labor and on consumption are not very large.

The heavier incidence of taxes on labor income than on capital income, though the difference is not substantial under the most progressive tax incidence assumptions, represents a major change from the relative tax burdens in 1966 (table 2.11). In 1966 capital income was taxed much more heavily than labor income for all income groups. The reversal depicted in the estimates for 1985 was due to both a moderate increase in the effective rate of taxes on labor income and a very large decline in the effective tax rate on capital income, reflecting, respectively, an increase in payroll tax rates and a decrease in capital gains, corporate income, and maximum personal income tax rates. Another interesting change in the structure of taxes over this twenty-year period is the decline in the progressiveness of taxes on labor income, reflecting mainly an increase in payroll tax rates. Whereas in 1966 tax rates on labor income, unlike those on capital and consumption, were fairly strongly progressive throughout the range of family income, by 1985 taxes on labor income evidenced considerably less progressivity. Thus the decline in progressiveness of all taxes combined over this period reflects both a decline in the progressiveness of taxes on labor income and, more important, a decrease in the relative burden of taxes on capital income, which is more heavily concentrated in the upper-income brackets.

There was not much difference in the relative importance of consumption taxes over this period. In both 1966 and 1980 the ratio of taxes on consumption to the level of consumption expenditures was roughly constant throughout the income scale; however, when these consumption taxes are expressed as a ratio to income, they are strongly

Table 2.11
Effective rates of combined federal, state, and local taxes on sources
and uses of income, under two sets of incidence assumptions, by
relative income ranking, 1966

Decile income group	Income from labor	Income from capital	Consumption taxes as a ratio of consumption
Most progressive incidence assumptions			
First[a]	11.8%	27.3%	6.8%
Second	13.8	26.0	7.7
Third	15.4	25.8	8.4
Fourth	15.9	26.0	8.5
Fifth	16.5	25.5	8.6
Sixth	16.6	24.7	8.6
Seventh	16.8	25.1	8.5
Eighth	17.1	26.2	8.6
Ninth	17.5	27.1	8.3
Tenth[b]	20.2	38.3	7.9
All	17.6	33.0	8.3
Least progressive incidence assumptions			
First[a]	10.0	22.0	16.1
Second	11.4	17.2	17.1
Third	13.2	18.1	17.7
Fourth	13.6	17.5	17.8
Fifth	14.3	17.1	17.7
Sixth	14.6	16.8	17.9
Seventh	14.9	17.6	18.0
Eighth	15.3	17.7	18.0
Ninth	15.8	17.8	17.8
Tenth[b]	19.3	23.5	17.0
All	16.0	21.0	17.6

Source: See table 2.5.
a. Includes only units in the sixth to tenth percentiles.
b. Excludes top 1 percent.

regressive. As a result a flat VAT or other flat consumption-based tax would be strongly regressive unless associated with offsetting tax measures. Their other major effect on the tax burden borne by different socioeconomic groups would be an increase in the relative burden of the younger and older families and a decrease in the burden of the middle-aged families (those with heads between 45 and 64 years of age).[32]

Impact of Corporate Taxes on Different Industries

The corporate tax currently is not a major source of federal revenues. Nonetheless there are differences in the effective tax rates among industries and among types of capital expenditures. The Economic Recovery Tax Act of 1981 widened these differences through differential tax reductions.

Tax Rates
The current maximum statutory corporate tax rate is 46.0 percent. From 1955 on the effective average tax rate based on economic income was, with the sole exception of 1974, less than the statutory rate (table 2.12). The average effective tax rate fell to 29.3 percent in 1982 and 28.8 percent in 1983, primarily due to the tax changes of the Reagan administration.[33] Economic income is measured here as reported corporate profits with inventory valuation and capital consumption adjustments.

There are wide differences among industries in average effective tax rates. Alan J. Auerbach estimated that for 1982 the average effective tax rate on existing capital varied across industries from 6.3 percent (water transportation) to 39.4 percent (water supply, sanitary services, and other institutions). These estimates are shown in table 2.13. Exactly who bears the burden of these taxes depends on the ability of firms to shift these taxes to consumers.

Table 2.12
Percentage corporate tax rates, 1955–1983

Year	Statutory rate	Average effective rate[a]	Difference
1955	52.0	48.0	4.0
1956	52.0	49.8	2.2
1957	52.0	48.7	3.3
1958	52.0	48.5	3.5
1959	52.0	46.8	5.2
1960	52.0	46.6	5.4
1961	52.0	46.0	6.0
1962	52.0	41.5	10.5
1963	52.0	41.2	10.8
1964	50.0	39.5	10.5
1965	48.0	37.5	10.5
1966	48.0	38.4	9.6
1967	48.0	37.9	10.1
1968	52.8	42.4	10.4
1969	52.8	44.4	8.4
1970	49.2	45.1	4.1
1971	48.0	42.8	5.2
1972	48.0	41.0	7.0
1973	48.0	42.9	5.1
1974	48.0	51.5	−3.5
1975	48.0	42.8	5.2
1976	48.0	43.8	4.2
1977	48.0	41.3	6.7
1978	48.0	40.9	7.1
1979	46.0	42.1	3.9
1980	46.0	44.6	1.4
1981	46.0	38.4	7.6
1982	46.0	29.3	16.7
1983	46.0	28.8	17.2

Source: *Economic Report of the President* (February 1984), tables B-82, and B-83; Alan J. Auerbach, "Corporate Taxation in the United States," Brookings Papers on Economic Activity 2 (Washington, D.C.: Brookings, 1983).
a. The profits and taxes of the Federal Reserve System are excluded.

Table 2.13
Effective tax rates, 1982

Industry number	Category	Tax rate
1	Food and kindred products	27.0
2	Tobacco manufacturers	24.3
3	Textile mill products	22.8
4	Apparel and other fabricated textile products	25.3
5	Paper and allied products	18.3
6	Printing, publishing, and allied industries	28.1
7	Chemicals and allied products	20.1
8	Petroleum and coal products	33.2
9	Rubber and miscellaneous plastic products	19.8
10	Leather and leather products	27.4
11	Lumber and wood products, except furniture	25.3
12	Furniture and fixtures	28.6
13	Stone, clay, and glass products	24.6
14	Primary metal industries	26.0
15	Fabricated metal industries	23.3
16	Machinery except electrical	24.6
17	Electrical machinery, equipment, and supplies	24.7
18	Transportation equipment, except motor vehicles and ordnance	30.4
19	Motor vehicles and motor vehicle equipment	21.3
20	Professional photographic equipment and watches	27.0
21	Miscellaneous manufacturing industries	25.8
22	Agricultural production	16.8
23	Agricultural services, horticultural services, forestry, and fisheries	14.7
24	Metal mining	34.3
25	Coal mining	19.1
26	Crude petroleum and natural gas extraction	32.2
27	Nonmetallic mining and quarrying, except fuel	15.6
28	Construction	13.1
29	Railroads and railway express service	21.4
30	Street railway, bus lines, and taxicab service	10.0

Table 2.13 (*continued*)

Industry number	Category	Tax rate
31	Trucking service, warehousing, and storage	14.7
32	Water transportation	6.3
33	Air transportation	11.5
34	Pipelines, except natural gas	22.9
35	Service incidental to transportation	17.1
36	Telephone, telegraph, and miscellaneous communication service	19.7
37	Radio broadcasting and television	25.8
38	Electric utilities	25.0
39	Gas utilities	20.0
40	Water supply, sanitary services and other utilities	39.4
41	Wholesale trade	18.7
42	Retail trade	27.5
43	Finance, insurance and real estate	37.3
44	Services	23.9

Source: Alan J. Auerbach, "Corporate Taxation in the United States," Brookings Papers on Economic Activity 2 (Washington, D.C.: Brookings, 1983), p. 468.

Although tax rates on existing capital are relevant for measuring the welfare implications of existing taxes, the appropriate rates to measure the effect of the corporate tax system on allocation of new investments are the effective tax rates on the new investments themselves. Ultimately, as the existing capital stock is replaced, these effective tax rates will become the effective tax rates on existing capital.

The average tax rates on new capital have always differed among industries, but the accelerated cost recovery system put into effect under the Reagan administration substantially increased the differences among industries. As an example, the Council of Economic Advisers in its 1982 report estimates that the motor vehicle industry had

Table 2.14
Effective tax rates on new depreciable assets, selected industries, 1982

Industry	Old law	New law
Agriculture	32.7	16.6
Mining	28.4	− 3.4
Primary metals	34.0	7.5
Machinery and instruments	38.2	18.6
Motor vehicles	25.8	− 11.3
Food	44.1	20.8
Pulp and paper	28.5	0.9
Chemicals	28.8	8.6
Petroleum refining	35.0	1.1
Transportation services	31.0	− 2.9
Utilities	43.2	30.6
Communications	39.8	14.1
Services and trade	53.2	37.1

Source: *Economic Report of the President* (February 1982).
Note: Industries chosen had at least $5 billion in new investment in 1981.
The table assumes a 4 percent real after-tax rate of return and 8 percent
inflation.

an effective tax rate of 25.8 percent on new capital under
the old law in comparison to − 11.3 percent under the new
law (table 2.14). Similarly mining and transportation services had negative rates on new investments. Although all
industries saw a reduction in their effective tax rates on
new investments, the resulting effective tax rates differed
substantially among industries, with services and trade
having the greatest effective tax rates on new investments.

The difference in the effective tax rates on new investments among industries hinges in a complex way on the
composition of the new investments, the assumed inflation rates, the method of financing, and the type of ownership. Using a model they developed, Mervyn King and
Don Fullerton estimated the effective tax rates on new investment cross-classified by inflation and various categories (table 2.15). Of particular note is the very favorable tax

Table 2.15
Effective marginal tax rates on capital income following the Tax Equity and Fiscal Responsibility Act of 1982

	Inflation rate		
Capital income	Zero	6.77	10.00
Asset			
Machinery	−0.3%	11.0%	15.7%
Buildings	27.4	33.2	34.7
Inventories	50.9	47.0	45.5
Industry			
Manufacturing	38.4	46.4	49.0
Other industry	7.9	11.4	12.4
Commerce	29.6	30.5	30.5
Financing			
Debt	−8.9	−23.5	−29.1
New issues of stock	57.8	87.7	101.2
Retained earnings	43.9	57.3	61.7
Owner			
Household	39.7	52.7	57.2
Tax-exempt institution	−3.5	−29.8	−45.3
Insurance company	−3.0	17.3	39.2
Overall	28.7	31.5	33.0

Source: Mervyn King and Don Fullerton, eds., "The United States," in *The Taxation of Income from Capital*, discussion paper no. 37 (Princeton: Princeton University, Woodrow Wilson School of Public and International Affairs, December 1982).

Note: Present value of federal income tax, state income tax, and state and local property tax paid as percentage of the return to $1 of additional investment on the part of all owners of the specified asset. (Assumes all investments begin with a 10 percent pretax return.) For an explanation of the economic model used to generate these results, see Mervyn King and Don Fullerton, eds., "The Theoretical Framework," in *The Taxation of Income from Capital: A Comparative Study of the U.S., U.K., Sweden and West Germany*, discussion paper no. 36 (Princeton: Princeton University, Woodrow Wilson School of Public and International Affairs, December 1982).

treatment of machinery at all levels of inflation relative to the tax treatment of investment in buildings and inventories.

Foreign Trade

The popular press frequently reports on favorable tax and other subsidies given by the Japanese to their export industries and about the rebating of the VAT on exports by European governments. It is alleged that these actions by foreign governments place U.S. firms at a disadvantage relative to foreign firms. The next chapter presents an economic analysis of the validity of these types of claims, with special reference to a floating exchange environment. This section outlines the general characteristics of the taxation of U.S. firms on their foreign activities and the taxation of foreign firms on their U.S. activities.

As a fundamental principle the U.S. government taxes the worldwide income of all domestic corporations as that income is earned; however, a subsidiary of a U.S. corporation incorporated in a foreign country is not viewed as a U.S. entity and thus does not have its earnings taxed when earned but only upon repatriation through the payments of dividends or royalties. This ability to defer U.S. taxes on nonrepatriated earnings will save U.S. corporations $1.0 billion in 1985. A U.S. corporation can take a tax credit for foreign taxes paid up to certain limits, roughly the U.S. tax liability on their foreign income. Thus if the foreign tax is less than the U.S. tax, U.S. corporations will have to pay a greater rate than foreign companies on the earnings that are repatriated. Indirect taxes such as VATs are not allowed as tax credits.

The ability to avoid paying U.S. taxes on earnings of foreign incorporated subsidiaries until repatriated has led to certain abuses. Subpart F of the 1962 Revenue Act caused controlled foreign corporations to recognize as

"deemed dividends" approximately the difference between the U.S. tax and the foreign tax. By declaring this
sum a dividend, the U.S. corporation would have to pay
U.S. tax on this amount even if the moneys were not repatriated at the time.

The United States provides tax incentives for exports
through domestic international sales corporations (so-
called DISCs). By setting up a separate entity for the exporting of domestic products, a corporation can realize
substantial tax advantages. The tax savings to corporations
are estimated to be $1.4 billion for 1985. Due to complaints
by the European community, the administration is propos-
ing foreign sales corporations (FSC) as a replacement for
DISCs. FSCs will receive about the same tax treatment as
DISCs.

Foreign corporations are taxed on their business activities in the United States at the usual corporate rates. To the
extent that most of the value-added occurs in the United
States, this provision will treat both U.S. and foreign firms
in similar ways; however, if much of the expense of the
U.S. sales represents intracompany purchases from a
foreign subsidiary, there is always the problem of correctly
determining the intracompany transfer price.

3

Basic Issues and Problems in Tax Policy

Issues

Equity

The primary objective of most taxation (abstracting from the relatively small amount of use taxes) is to raise the revenues required to finance the government expenditures perceived as necessary for the public welfare. In the short run government expenditures can be financed also by debt, but in the longer run they must depend largely on tax revenues to ensure a healthy, noninflationary economy. The main issues in tax as distinguished from expenditures policy revolve about how to distribute the burden of taxation as equitably and efficiently as possible.

For taxation to be equitable, it must be perceived as being fair. Specifically people with identical real income (per equivalent adult) and other similar relevant family circumstances would be expected to pay the same level of taxes (horizontal equity), while people with different economic means would be expected to pay taxes consistent with their ability to pay (vertical equity). For taxes to be efficient, they must be raised so as to minimize distortions in the allocation of economic resources (allocational efficiency), minimize the social costs of collection (operational efficiency), and to the extent possible contribute to economic growth and stability of total output by maintaining appropriate labor and capital incentives.

Horizontal equity is a goal of taxation that is almost universally agreed on. Apart from political pressures by special interest groups, this goal is relatively easy to implement once it is decided what economic activity—income earned, goods and services consumed, or wealth held—should be taxed. Traditionally income has been regarded as the best measure of ability to pay taxes and the fairest basis of assessing a taxpayer's share of the costs of government services. Income taxes have dominated tax collection in the United States, especially at the federal level. In recent years an increasing number of economists have argued for the economic superiority of some form of consumption over income taxes, but most economists, including many who prefer consumption taxes on efficiency grounds, believe that equity considerations require that individuals or families with the same economic means pay the same taxes. Some economists now argue that the amount of resources that a taxpayer consumes is a better standard to measure progressivity on the argument that two taxpayers with the same level of consumption receive the same benefits from society regardless of their income.

Economic considerations might, of course, argue for a different distribution of taxes from that based solely on equity considerations as a result of uneven effects of certain taxes on labor and investment incentives; however, unless the economic advantages are so compelling that virtually all taxpayers would be at least as well off as a result, it is difficult to justify departures from horizontal equity. The current tax structure embodies numerous departures from such equity, apparently reflecting among other things a desire to stimulate or to discourage certain forms of economic activity (for example, investment in business equipment versus gasoline consumption) or simply difficulties of measurement (such as imputed income on owned homes and unrealized real capital gains).

The definition of income appropriate to ensure equity of the tax burden is closer to the concept of economic income, which would include real capital gains, than to the somewhat narrower concept of taxable income mandated by law. Totally apart from the problem of determining the appropriate time horizon for measuring income, there are a number of other difficulties in equating the real before-tax disposable income of different families, including adjustment for family size, for abnormal medical and other work-related expenditures deemed necessary for earning income, for significant regional differences in the cost of living, and so forth. Although there is no universal agreement on the fairest disposition of all these difficulties, they are generally susceptible to reasonable solutions.

Although total income is usually taken to be the best measure of economic means or ability to pay taxes, the source of income might also be considered relevant to a person's economic means or ability to pay taxes. The capitalized value of income from capital, which is a marketable form of wealth, is associated with greater potential purchasing power than the capitalized value of income from labor, which is a nonmarketable form of wealth. From the viewpoint of economic theory it can be argued that the total of human and nonhuman wealth is a better measure of economic means than total income from labor and capital and that the appropriate wealth multiple for labor income is smaller than that for capital income. The return from human wealth is normally riskier than that from nonhuman wealth or net worth since human wealth is nonmarketable and reflects a largely nondiversifiable form of risk.[1] As a result, it can be argued, the application of the same rate of taxation to labor and capital income represents a somewhat higher burden for labor than for capital.

Although the concept of horizontal equity poses no

significant problem other than the measurement of income and related economic variables, the concept of vertical equity is largely dependent on matters of subjective judgment. Specifically there is no generally accepted ethical standard (and certainly no economic standard) that casts much light on the appropriate comparative ratios of taxes to income in different income groups. Perhaps the only reasonably general point of agreement on equity grounds found among economists and noneconomists alike is that the effective tax rates in upper-income classes should be at least as high as those in lower-income groups. People who believe on social or philosophical grounds that taxation should be used to reduce the before-tax concentration of income in the upper-income classes would favor a more progressive tax structure, but such matters are subjective in nature and have no economic or other scientific justification.[2] We shall assume, however, that any major changes in the tax system should at least not convert the present relatively flat level of effective tax rates across incomes into a regressive structure. This would seem to be a minimum requirement on grounds of both generally agreed equity considerations and political acceptability.

One other implicit equity issue is associated with any major changes in the tax system, no matter how desirable in the long run. If such changes are disruptive to current capital values, they may lead to very substantial, and it could be argued unwarranted, capital gains or losses to large sectors of the population. Thus treating capital gains as ordinary income would significantly lower common stock prices unless offsetting changes were enacted. Eliminating the federal income tax exemptions from future state and local government bonds or from imputed rental income on owned houses would raise the value of existing tax exempts and lower both the value of houses and the favorable tax treatment of home owners. A switch from a major reliance on income taxes to consumption taxes would, at least initially, favor property income and values at the expense of labor income. Clearly appropriate transitional steps would have to be considered, which might mean stretching out the transition period or enacting special one-time taxes or subsidies.

Efficiency Issues in Tax Policy

Both the level and composition of taxes can profoundly affect the functioning of the economy. Taxes not only divert resources from private to public use but also influence the manner in which the resources available to the private sector are utilized. This study does not focus on the important questions relating to the optimal total levels of government expenditures and taxes but only on those relating to the optimal structure of taxes given total government outlays and taxes.

The structure of taxes can affect the functioning of the economy in many areas, notably including the efficiency of the allocation of resources to different outputs, saving and investment behavior, the labor supply, the stock market, other financial markets, the form and capital structure of business, and investor portfolios. The most important of these effects are those that affect the level and growth of the real national output. Here we summarize the theoretical and empirical literature concerning two of the tax structure effects on real economic activity that have received the most attention in recent years: those on realized savings and investment and those on the labor supply.

Saving and Investment Incentives

Perhaps most stress in criticisms of the tax structure over the past decade has been laid on its alleged excess taxation of income on capital. Such an imbalance has been cited as contributing to a low ratio of net savings and capital formation to the national income, resulting in a low rate of economic growth. In recent years there also has been increasing attention paid to the potentially adverse effect of taxation of wages and salaries on the labor supply. Since it is not feasible to cut taxes on capital income without raising them on labor income (or vice-versa), while holding total taxes and government expenditures constant, the implications for economic efficiency of offsetting changes in the two types of taxes would depend on the tax sensitivities of the consumption-saving and labor-leisure choices.[3] However, it should be noted that the analysis in chapter 2 of the burden of taxation on different sources of income indicated that, as a result of changes in the tax structure over the last ten to twenty years, capital income is no longer taxed more heavily than labor income (tables 2.10 and 2.11). In fact the most current estimates of tax burden, if taken at face value, imply that for most income groups labor income is somewhat more heavily taxed than capital income.[4]

It is conceivable that the economy would be better off with an even lower relative burden of taxes on capital if the supply of capital is much more tax sensitive than is the supply of labor.[5] Although there is no consensus among economists about the after-tax return elasticities of private or aggregate saving, however, our own assessment is that neither the relevant theory nor the empirical evidence provides much support for the belief that higher after-tax rates of return on assets stimulate the private sector's propensity to save.[6] There is evidence that a redistribution of after-tax income from the lower- to the upper-income groups, regardless of the form it takes, would increase the private sector's saving-income ratio at least in the short or intermediate run though not necessarily in the long run.[7] Thus it might be possible to stimulate the aggregate propensity to save by shifting the overall burden of taxation (on both labor and capital incomes) from the upper- to the lower-income groups, but there is no strong evidence that the effect on saving of this regressive shift would be either large or sustained. A shift in taxation from corporations to individuals would probably increase the aggregate propensity to save, at least in the short and intermediate run, in view of the substantially higher propensity to save by corporations than by individuals.[8] Yet the fairly pronounced shift in taxes of recent years from capital to labor income, together with the general decline in the progressiveness of the tax structure, especially for the top income group, was associated with a decline in the ratios to income of personal, private, and total saving to their lowest levels since the post–World War II adjustment in the late 1940s. This was true in spite of the specific additional saving incentives provided by IRA, Keogh, and similar plans.

Although the impact of capital income taxes on saving behavior by an after-tax return effect is not entirely clear, even in direction, both theory and empirical evidence seem to indicate a negative impact of the cost of capital on investment.[9] For risky investment, however, the cost of capital is not necessarily positively related, as might be expected, to the level of income taxes. Theoretical considerations do suggest a positive effect of higher corporate income taxes on the cost of capital and hence a negative effect on stock prices and investment; however, this is not necessarily true of higher personal income taxes, at least in the short run, since under certain plausible assumptions (including personal tax credits for investment losses) investor risk is decreased more than expected return.[10] On the other hand both empirical and theoretical evidence point to a positive relation between the cost of capital and the level of corporate income taxation and hence a negative relation between the cost of capital and the magnitude of investment tax credits and depreciation deductions. Even here, however, the effectiveness of changes in corporation income taxation on investment would be limited in the long run by the apparent long-run ineffectiveness of such changes on saving incentives.

Combining these different strands of theoretical and empirical evidence relating to the separate effects of capital income taxation (corporate and personal) on saving and investment behavior, our judgment is that a reduction of capital income taxes, especially at the corporate level, would stimulate investment over the cycle, but the long-run effect on capital formation is likely to be moderate if our assessment of the apparently low after-tax interest elasticity of saving is correct. Maximizing the effect on investment would require strongly regressive changes in the tax structure such as might be effected by the combination of eliminating corporate income taxes and either raising taxes on labor income or substituting a flat consumption tax for progressive income taxes. Such changes would probably raise corporations' propensity to invest both in the short and long run and stimulate aggregate saving at least in the short and intermediate run, in view of the higher saving propensity of the upper-income groups. Thus it is possible but by no means certain that a significant increase in capital formation could be effected, at least for a number of years, by a substantial increase in the regressiveness of the tax structure.

In the long run, however, the apparently low after-tax interest elasticity of saving would limit any increase in capital formation that might be associated with a more regressive tax structure. Moreover any beneficial effect of a more regressive tax structure on economic growth as a result of the stimulation of investment might be depressed at least in part by weakened labor incentives as the lower taxes on capital income are financed by higher taxes on labor income.

Labor Incentives
Totally apart from the quantitative uncertainty of the outcome, two problems are raised by more favorable taxation of income on capital and of the upper-income groups generally. The first concerns equity in the distribution of the burden of taxes among different sectors of the population. The second concerns the higher rates of taxation on labor income and the consequently depressed labor incentives that a reduction in capital income taxes might require. Although there is conflicting evidence on the quantitative effect of taxes on the labor supply, most recent studies imply at least some negative after-tax elasticity. Furthermore there is no obvious reason for believing on the basis of either theoretical or empirical considerations that labor is any less sensitive to taxes than saving and, hence in the long run, investment; in fact it may well be more sensitive.[11] The estimated responsiveness of labor supply to income taxation varies widely among studies depending on the methodology used. The response is quite small when judged by the results of survey interviews and only moderately higher according to most econometric analyses. The degree of responsiveness by married women, not surprisingly, generally is found to be significantly higher than that by their working husbands. The substantial rise in the real wage rate over more than a century, which has been associated with a marked reduction in hours worked, has also been cited as evidence against an important positive income effect on the labor supply. Such a trend, however, is not necessarily inconsistent with a significant positive marginal after-tax income effect on the labor supply.[12]

Our interpretation of the state of the art does not indicate any major beneficial effects on economic incentives resulting from a shift in taxes either from capital to labor income or from upper- to lower-income groups; however, we believe that taxes do pose disincentives to the form of economic activity being taxed. Although there is no certainty about their quantitative importance, in our judgment these effects are moderate in size.

An obvious approach to diminishing the disruptive effects on both labor and capital of a given total of taxation would be to minimize the marginal rates of taxation paid on income, keeping them consistent with a desired rate of progressivity in the average tax-income ratios. As long as the desired rate of progressivity in average tax rates is not too high, it is quite feasible to have an increase in average tax rates with increasing income levels without imposing extremely high marginal rates at any income level.

In connection with the discussion of the effects of taxation on economic activity, there does not appear to be a solid basis to the common assertion that the unsatisfactory rate of capital formation and economic growth in the United States as compared to other Western countries and Japan can be mostly attributed to our high taxes on income from capital. The most careful comparative study in this area concludes, on the basis of an admittedly limited sample of five countries: "Germany has the highest overall effective tax on income from capital *and* the highest growth rate. The U.S. is second in both categories and Sweden is third. The U.K. has the lowest overall effective tax on income from capital *and* the lowest growth rate. If we look at growth of nonfinancial corporate capital, results are substantially the same. The U.S. and Sweden are reversed, but Germany is still the highest and Britain is the lowest."[13] Lower marginal rates of taxation on capital and labor incomes probably do contribute to investment and work incentives, but their effectiveness should not be exaggerated.

The substitution of flat consumption taxes (such as a value-added tax or sales tax) for progressive income taxes probably would stimulate aggregate saving moderately, at least in the short run and perhaps even for longer. Flat consumption taxes might, on the other hand, have larger effects than income taxes on labor incentives. The effect on saving and labor incentives of two other types of personal taxes will be considered here since the general desirability of such taxes will be discussed subsequently in connection with an examination of the major proposed changes in the current tax structure. These two changes are the introduction of a comprehensive system of progressive consumption taxes and a greatly increased reliance on estate taxes.

The substitution of progressive consumption taxes for progressive income taxes would be expected to stimulate saving even less than the substitution of flat consumption taxes for progressive income taxes; however, progressive consumption taxes might have a modest stimulating effect on saving (reduce saving disincentives somewhat) as compared with retention of the present system.[14] Although there is little empirical basis for estimating the effect on saving of the partial substitution of higher estate taxes for income taxes, such an effect probably would be quite small as long as the progressivity of the taxes is similar. Similarly, we would expect that the substitution of higher estate taxes for progressive income taxes would cut down modestly the disincentive effect of taxation on the labor supply, but the effect in any case would be quite small. There is no strong evidence on the disincentive effects of consumption and estate taxes on capital formation and labor supply, but the recent fairly substantial reduction in estate taxes had no discernable effect on capital formation or labor incentives.

Allocational Efficiency

Conceptually a major purpose of taxation and government expenditures is to alter the allocation of resources from the competitive allocation that would have occurred without the government. Where social benefits and costs differ from private benefits and costs, the intervention of the government in the private sector makes possible an overall improvement in the allocation of resources. For example, police, courts, and military provide stability to the domestic and international sectors, thereby enhancing the productivity of the private sector. Quite apart from productivity considerations, most people believe that the government may properly intervene in the private sector to redistribute income and wealth for equity reasons.

The role of the government here is to improve the overall welfare of society, and the principal tools are taxes and expenditures. Thus even if it were theoretically and empirically possible, a comparison of the allocation of resources with the government to that without the government would shed little light on tax policy itself. A more pragmatic and perhaps more useful way to evaluate tax policy is to compare actual taxes on different sources of income to a base case in which the tax system treats all sources of income equally. Except for reasons of social policy or for enhancing the productivity of the private sector, most economists would support the proposition that tax policy should not make one source of income more desirable to a taxpayer for tax reasons than another source. This proposition is consistent with the view of horizontal equity.

The personal income tax treats some forms of income more favorably than other types. Examples include the lower taxation of long-term capital gains, the favorable treatment of home ownership, and the exclusion of municipal bond interest. Such differential tax treatments affect the way in which individual investors allocate their savings and wealth. Unless there are compelling reasons to believe that such differential tax treatments increase the productivity of the private sector, economic arguments by themselves provide no justification for continuing such differentials. In addition such differentials almost certainly will lead to violations of horizontal equity. The justification for such differential tax treatments must rest primarily on social and public policy considerations.

Except for housing, individuals generally do not undertake directly new investments; rather they undertake investments indirectly through financial intermediaries or financial assets. Thus the corporate tax as it affects the investment decisions of managers becomes an important determinant of how resources are allocated. Corporate taxes vary substantially from one type of undertaking to another.

Alan J. Auerbach presents an excellent discussion of the sources of the potential distortionary effects of the corporate tax. In recent years marginal tax rates on new investments in the form of equipment have been less than those on new investments in the form of buildings, possibly affecting the technological form of new investments.[15] Depending on the past history of earnings, two firms evaluating the same investment may face different marginal tax rates due to their differential ability to utilize past losses as income offsets or to carry forward current losses.[16] The portion of debt used to finance a new investment will influence the attractiveness of the investment due to the deductibility of interest. The value of this deduction hinges in a complicated way on expected inflation and the likelihood that a firm will have sufficient future profits to utilize the deduction.

The potential distortionary effects of the federal tax code are manifold, and one can always add further potential effects to any list. What is important for policy is the magnitude of the distortions, not the number of distortions. The distortions from taxing income from different sources at vastly different rates depend on the production technology, the mobility of the work force, the substitutability of labor for capital, the distribution of personal wealth, and the substitutability of one consumer product for another.

In a series of important and influential papers, Arnold Harberger analyzed a two-sector model with one sector heavily taxed and the other lightly taxed.[17] He applied his model to national income data from 1953 to 1959, a period when the corporate tax exceeded the noncorporate tax. His conclusion was that the higher corporate tax reduced overall income by 0.5 to 1.0 percent of GNP from what it would have been under an equal tax on both sectors.[18] John Shoven found similar distortions using a twelve-sector model.[19] In view of the much-reduced taxes in the corporate sector in recent years, one should be very cautious in extrapolating these estimates to today's economy. As an additional distortion Auerbach more recently has estimated that the different tax treatment of equipment and structures reduced national income by some $5 billion in 1981, considerably less than 1 percent of GNP.[20] This number probably is upward biased because he does not consider the tax advantages of the debt capacity associated with structures, nor does he recognize the discretion of an accountant to classify parts of structures as equipment. Nonetheless Auerbach's analysis and the earlier analyses of Harbinger and Shoven indicate that the corporate tax has a measurable distortionary effect on the economy.

The magnitude of the distortion, of course, depends on the base to which the forgone output is compared. In this regard Shoven has argued that the size of the distortion should not be measured relative to GNP but rather to the tax that is collected.[21] Using a much smaller base gives a much bigger percentage.

Following Shoven's logic, the proper measure of the revenues raised through the corporate tax is the gross tax less the costs of the distortions. Making this adjustment to today's numbers would reduce further the already small importance of corporate tax revenues. If corporate taxes continue to decline, it is possible, if it has not already happened, that the costs of the distortions introduced by this tax could well exceed the gross tax collected.

Costs of Compliance

The costs of compliance represent still another tax cost borne by the economy: the costs associated with the preparation of tax forms and related reporting requirements by households and business firms and the costs of ensuring compliance with the relevant laws by government agencies. As tax rates have risen historically and tax forms have become increasingly complex, reflecting a vast array of full or partial tax exemptions for different types of income and expenditures, the direct and indirect costs of tax compliance have grown substantially, though it is extremely difficult to obtain reliable estimates.

Such costs are likely to be most important for income taxes, where the opportunities for legally or illegally minimizing taxes are likely to offer sufficiently large financial incentives to compensate taxpayers for a significant expenditure of their own time and frequently for out-of-pocket payment to outside experts. These imputed and monetary costs of taxpayer compliance are related to such activities as record keeping, making appropriate investment decisions, estimating taxes under alternative permissible practices, keeping up with relevant changes in the tax laws and rules, and on occasion being involved in audit procedures. These compliance costs are in addition to the allocational inefficiencies associated with the uneven tax treatment of different economic activities.

Perhaps the best, though still rough, estimates of the magnitude of the compliance costs associated with federal and state individual income taxes are those made for Minnesota by Joel Slemrod and by Slemrod together with

Nikki Sorum.[22] Based on a survey of Minnesota taxpayers in 1982, these authors conclude that for the United States as a whole in that year, the compliance costs of filing federal and state individual income tax returns amounted to between $17 billion and $27 billion, or from 5 to 7 percent of the income tax revenues raised. Of these totals it is estimated that $3.0 billion to $3.4 billion was spent on professional tax assistance; the remainder represented the imputed cost of between 1.8 billion to 2.1 billion hours of taxpayer time spent on filing tax returns. Adding in the resources used by the collection agencies and third parties (primarily employers withholding taxes), Slemrod concludes that a conservative estimate of total collection costs is 7 to 8 percent of total revenues, or about $30 billion annually.[23]

Simplification of the income tax laws could reduce compliance costs, though it is not clear by how much. A shift in the structure of U.S. taxes from income toward VAT or sales taxes probably would also reduce compliance costs, but this might be less true of a shift toward progressive consumption taxes. Some insight into the magnitude of possible savings in compliance costs by simplification of individual income taxes is provided by Slemrod. He estimates on the basis of his survey results that the elimination of itemized deductions would reduce the total resource costs of compliance by about 6.5 percent. On the other hand his results suggest that a single-rate or flat income tax structure, which is one of the major tax proposals currently under consideration, would not change significantly the costs of compliance. This finding may, as Slemrod notes, reflect the inadequacies of the available data, but it is supported by a fairly detailed, though largely qualitative, analysis by Joseph A. Minarik.[24] Unfortunately no information is available to our knowledge on compliance costs associated with the preparation of corporate income tax returns. Clearly they are significant but probably not as large in the aggregate as compliance costs for individual income tax returns.

Although with other things equal it would be desirable to minimize compliance costs, the limited evidence available does not necessarily associate very large savings with specific changes in the income tax structure, unless they were to entail the replacement of the entire system of individual or corporate income taxes with a much less costly alternative such as might be provided by some forms of consumption-based taxes. The integration of the corporate income tax into the individual income tax might also result in substantial savings. The desirability of changes in the U.S. tax structure is likely to depend more on their effects on perceived equity among taxpayers and on economic efficiency than on compliance costs.

Foreign Trade

A major determinant of the general attractiveness of U.S.-made products to foreign buyers is the exchange rate between the dollar and the foreign currency. Assume, for example, that there is only one traded good, its export price as delivered in the foreign land is $100, and the price of that good produced in the foreign land is 400 units of the foreign currency. If the exchange rate is 4 units of the foreign currency per dollar, the exported good will be competitive. In this case there is purchasing power parity between the two currencies.

Before analyzing more realistic models, let us examine what would happen if the foreign government began to subsidize the domestic manufacturers of this product and thereby reduced its price to 350 units of foreign currency. For purchasing power parity to remain, the exchange rate must change to 3.5 units of the foreign currency per dollar. Thus movements in the exchange rate will neutralize the subsidy.

Indeed in this simple scenario movements in the exchange rate will neutralize any differences in national tax rates. Thus the inability of U.S. corporations to use VATs that are paid in Europe as tax credits on income repatriated to the United States should have no lasting impact on the competitiveness of U.S. products in foreign markets.

Let us now examine the more realistic case in which there are multiple goods traded between the United States and a foreign country. If the tax rates were the same for all industries within each of the countries, although not necessarily the same between the countries, the exchange rates would tend to adjust so that the United States would export goods in which it held a comparative advantage and import goods in which the foreign country held a comparative advantage. Both countries would be better off. If, however, the United States or the foreign country were to impose different tax rates or subsidies on different industries, the relative attractiveness of its exported goods to the foreign country will change. Changes in exchange rates cannot undo such differential tax treatment. Changes in exchange rates can undo only across-the-board tax changes. Thus the United States should strive to maintain the same effective tax rates by industry and persuade foreign countries to do the same. Maintaining equal tax treatment across industries is desirable even without foreign trade and is essential for allocational efficiency in the United States and for horizontal equity.

Although foreign exchange rates gravitate over time to purchasing power parity, sometimes they can deviate from parity by substantial margins. Foreign investors may view investments in the United States as very attractive from risk and return considerations and thereby bid up the dollar, as is happening today, with the record high real interest rates in the U.S. and a comparatively stable political system. When the dollar is overvalued relative to purchasing power, foreign firms will find it easier to sell their products in the United States and U.S. firms will find it more difficult to sell their products in foreign lands. While true, these observations have little to do with the corporate tax system itself.

Countercyclical Features

In discussing countercyclical functions of a tax system, it is customary and useful to distinguish between the automatic stabilizing nature of the tax and discretionary uses of the tax. A tax system serves as an automatic stabilizer when cyclical movements in the economy have smaller amplitudes because of its presence, without government taking any specific actions for the purpose. Thus the income tax serves as an automatic stabilizer because when the total aggregate demand in the economy fluctuates, the tax revenue moves more than proportionately with aggregate demand so that income after taxes fluctuates less than proportionately. Real estate taxes, in contrast, being relatively constant in the short run, make income after taxes fluctuate more than proportionately with the aggregate demand. Consumption taxes are intermediate between the two.

A discretionary use of a tax, on the other hand, requires an explicit action of the government on each occasion. For example, the temporary surcharge on personal and corporate income taxes was imposed by the administration and the Congress in 1968 explicitly to counter the overly stimulated conditions of the economy. A rebate on personal income taxes was given in 1975 in order to counter the severe recession in 1975.

In the past, both in practice and in the academic literature, attention has been focused on the ability of taxes to moderate fluctuations of the aggregate demand. In order to lay out the function of the tax system as an automatic

Table 3.1
Relation of GNP to personal disposable income for 1982 (billions)

GNP			$3,073
Less:	Capital consumption allowance with capital consumption adjustment		359
Equals:	Net national product		2,714
Less:	Indirect business tax and nontax liability		258
	Business transfer payments		14
	Statistical discrepancy		
Plus:	Subsidies less current surplus of government enterprises		10
Equals:	National income		2,450
Less:	Corporate profits with inventory valuation and capital consumption adjustments		165
	Net interest		261
	Contribution to social insurance		253
Plus:	Government transfer payments to persons		360
	Personal interest income		366
	Personal dividend income		66
	Business transfer payments		14
Equals:	Personal income		2,579
Less:	Personal tax and nontax payments		405
	Federal government		
	Income taxes	297	
	Estate and gift taxes	8	
	Nontaxes		
	State and local government		
	Income taxes	52	
	Nontaxes	36	
	Other	9	
Equals:	Disposable income		2,174

Source: *Survey of Current Business* 63 (July 1983); tables 1.7, 1.8, 1.11, 2.7, 3.2, 3.3.

stabilizer, it is useful to consider the relationship between GNP and disposable personal income, as shown in table 3.1. To the extent that any additive item listed between GNP and disposable personal income fluctuates less than proportionately with GNP when GNP fluctuates (more than proportionately with GNP if it is a subtraction item), such an item moderates the fluctuation of disposable income for a given fluctuation of GNP. The opposite proposition is also true.

The first tax item listed in table 3.1 is indirect business tax and nontax liability. Indirect business tax consists largely of real estate tax and excise taxes. Real estate tax is unresponsive to fluctuations of output and employment, while excise taxes tend to fluctuate more or less proportionately in response to fluctuations of aggregate demand.[25] Thus total indirect business taxes fluctuate less than proportionately in response to fluctuations of GNP, and hence they make net national product fluctuate more than proportionately with GNP when the latter fluctuates.

The next important tax is the corporate income or profit tax. Within a short period corporate profits are largely a residual, given the sales of corporations. The average cost, especially the capital cost and to a lesser extent the labor cost, cannot be reduced quickly when sales decline, so that corporate profits fluctuate proportionately much more than sales of corporations. Furthermore since dividends are fairly stable over time, undistributed profits are even more volatile.[26] This means that a large part of the cyclical fluctuation of national income is absorbed into undistributed corporate profits and corporate profit taxes, reducing cyclical fluctuations of personal income.

Corporate profit tax, which responds more or less proportionately to profits before tax, helps to reduce the absolute size of cyclical fluctuations of corporate profits after tax. What contributes to reducing cyclical fluctuations of personal income, however, are the characteristics of corporate profits, not of the corporate profit tax.

Under current theories of the behavior of households and corporations, both are supposed to base their decisions on the long-term, permanent characteristics of their environment and not on sudden, unexpected realization of random variables such as income and profits; however, these theories apply to firms and households that are not subject to short-run cash constraints and credit rationing. Also it is possible that under certain conditions, short-run cyclical fluctuations of profits or income may cause corporate managers and households to alter their expectations of future demand and income prospects fairly substantially. It is not possible here to review carefully all reasons and evidence for expecting individuals to be likely to react more substantially than corporations when a given amount of cyclical variation is shifted from corporate profits to personal income. We believe, however, that on the whole the response of households' consumption expenditure to fluctuations of their income will be larger than that of corporate investment to fluctuations of the same size in their profits.

It is unclear whether corporate profit tax as it is currently structured has any countercyclical influence on investment expenditure of corporations. If anything, it is probably procyclical, since an investment tax credit is worth more to corporations when there are ample profits and tax on profits against which corporations can take the credit. This does not mean that we cannot redesign some aspects of the corporate profit tax so that it would have strong countercyclical features by essentially making the investment less costly in recession and more costly under conditions of excess demand. But such a redesign probably would make the tax more complex, and in addition roughly the same effect might be accomplished by judicious use of monetary policies.

The next item in the table is contribution for social insurance. Currently it is mildly procyclical because it is regressive due to the fact that only wages and salaries up to a certain maximum are subject to tax. It can be made largely neutral from the countercyclical point of view by making all compensation subject to tax, while reducing the rate of contribution in order to keep the total revenue generated by this tax the same. This tax, especially the employer contributions part of it, is a potentially useful instrument in dealing with supply disturbances.

Although we are primarily concerned with taxes, in the discussion of stabilization policies it is necessary to touch briefly on the role of transfer payments. Transfer payments are actually negative taxes. The largest part of the federal government transfer payments (approximately $270 billion) is for old-age, survivor's, and disability insurance, hospital and supplementary medical insurance (Medicare), government employee retirement benefits, and veterans' benefits. This part of transfer payments is only marginally countercyclical, mainly because it enables older workers to retire early rather than face the possibility of the loss of their jobs. Of the remainder, unemployment benefits ($24 billion) and direct relief ($17 billion) are most countercyclical. Food stamp benefits ($10 billion) are also responsive to cyclical conditions but not as much as the unemployment insurance.

This brings us to personal income, and the last and the largest of taxes, personal income tax and nontax payments, of which the federal personal income tax is the dominant component. Since the federal personal income tax rate structure is progressive, it is tempting to conclude that it should be strongly countercyclical. In reality although it is mildly countercyclical, its strength has dissipated greatly in the past twenty years. The progressivity of rates in the federal income tax structure is being circumvented through a variety of loopholes, most of which are available only to wealthy individuals and families, so that the progressiveness of the actual tax system beyond the first few brackets does not seem to be very noticeable. In the 1950s and early 1960s the most important source of the progressivity of the federal personal income tax system was the personal exemption, which, at $600 per person, was roughly one-third of per capita personal income in 1955 ($1,878). The personal exemption now in force of $1,000 is less than one-tenth of per capita income in 1982 ($11,109). Consequently in the 1950s and early 1960s, when personal income rose (fell) by 1 percent, the federal personal income tax receipts rose (fell) by 1.5 percent, but now under the same circumstances the federal personal income tax receipts would rise (fall) by 1.2 percent or so. Most revisions of the tax system that have taken place since 1960 have reduced the marginal tax rates for each bracket, reflecting a rise in the level of personal exemption by a factor of two while the level of per capita income rose by a factor of ten. These revisions, together with a number of additional preferential treatments incorporated into the system, have reduced the countercyclical ability of this tax while shifting much of the burden of the tax from the relatively high income group to the relatively low income group.

We now turn to the discussion of discretionary uses of these tax systems. It is sometimes suggested that discretionary uses of fiscal instruments can never be relied on because, after the need for action is recognized, it takes too much time to formulate the legislative program to have committee hearings and final votes in both houses of Congress and then to work out a compromise between the Senate and the House version before any action can take place. Although this is quite often the case, it is not necessary, and once in a while, when the need was felt to be very great, the whole action was completed within three or four weeks.

Traditionally the most frequent discretionary actions using taxes are surcharges or temporary reductions in income taxes, mostly personal income taxes but including corporate profit taxes. We do not believe that a temporary shift of corporate profit tax is effective in reducing cyclical fluctuations of the economy. On the effectiveness of temporary changes in personal income tax, there is a controversy between those who believe that such changes are transmitted substantially into consumption expenditures by households and those who believe in the strict version of the permanent income hypothesis and therefore conclude that such temporary countercyclical shifts of taxes are largely averaged out by households in arriving at their notion of permanent income, and hence their effectiveness is minimal. It is difficult to settle this dispute with empirical evidence because these temporary shifts have not been very frequent and their size has not been large. To the extent that the evidence is available, it appears that the proportion of changes in income induced by these temporary tax changes utilized for consumption expenditure is somewhat less than the proportion of normal level of income utilized for consumption expenditure and that these changes in taxes are transmitted into consumption rather slowly over a period of one to two years.

In general the effect of discretionary countercyclical changes in those taxes that affect incomes tends to be mild, while consequences of temporary changes in those taxes that affect relative prices can be quite pronounced, but unfortunately their magnitude can be quite erratic. A temporary reduction in sales tax, for instance, may induce customers to take advantage of temporarily lowered prices during the affected period and attempt to purchase as much goods as possible, especially storable goods, thus inducing a large shift in timing of consumption. But it may be that for total consumption over a somewhat longer period, affecting relative prices can generate rather unexpected shifts and hence must be used with extreme caution.

Our discussion of the effectiveness of discretionary countercyclical tax changes is contingent on the assumption that monetary policy remains accommodating to the purpose for which these discretionary changes of taxes are undertaken. If the fiscal policy and monetary policy are aimed at diametrically opposite purposes, then the consequences of such a situation depend on the relative strength of both policies and cannot be predicted in general. Furthermore such conflicting policies pursued simultaneously can create serious allocational problems in the economy and may prove to be quite costly in the long run.

We now wish to comment briefly on tax structures and discretionary changes in them that are designed to reduce the severity of supply disturbances. Historically major supply disturbances large enough to disrupt the economy significantly have been quite rare, but a series of very large supply disturbances occurred in the 1970s, beginning with the consequences of the major dollar devaluation, followed by food shortages caused by poor harvests in the Soviet Union and parts of Africa and Asia, a raw materials shortage of 1973, and finally the oil crises of 1973–1974 and 1979–1980. This series of supply disturbances is an important contributing factor to the stagflation of the economy throughout most of the world.

Because these supply disturbances in the United States have tended to be much less frequent than demand disturbances, traditional designs of the tax system usually emphasize its ability to moderate the effects of demand disturbances, and little attention is paid to moderating supply disturbances. Since most supply disturbances involve a shift in relative prices, it is more difficult to design macrofiscal policy responses that would help moderate the effects of supply disturbances than designing policies to deal with demand disturbances. It is possible, however, to organize a series of fiscal actions that would substantially improve the economy's ability to adjust to supply disturbances, especially very large and sudden ones such as the first oil shock.

The effect of a supply disturbance such as the oil shock is to raise dramatically the price of oil to users. Since initially the rest of the prices in the economy, including the wage rate, do not rise, the second effect of such a shock is that the real income in the economy is suddenly and substantially reduced. This leads to a marked reduction in aggregate demand and an attempt to make up for the lost income by raising wage rates and eventually prices of other goods, creating stagflation.

The proper fiscal response in such a situation is to take actions that have the effect of reducing prices generally (rather than that for oil itself) and increasing aggregate demand at the same time. Some reduction in the rate of contribution to the social security system, especially employer contribution, has the required characteristics. We could use general sales taxes or a VAT at the federal level.

The use of the social security contribution for this type of purpose is not different from the use of any other tax for a similar purpose from a purely economic point of view. Given the perception of the public that the social security system is a separate entity from the rest of the federal budget, it may create serious political problems. These could be mitigated by providing the social security system with a reasonable alternative source of funds. For example, in the case of the oil shock, we could have let the domestic price of oil rise to the world level immediately after the first oil shock, impose a windfall profit tax on domestic producers as we eventually did, and specify that the proceeds of the windfall profit tax be channeled into the social security system. Then we could determine the size of the social security contribution reduction so that the total revenue of the system remains roughly unchanged. We do not necessarily advocate this particular program as the best one to deal with supply disturbances, but we offer it here in order to demonstrate that some such design is possible and that the series of supply disruptions of the 1970s could have been handled substantially more effectively than it was.

Most of the discussion here assumes that the fiscal and monetary policies are being designed to serve the same purpose and that they do not work at cross-purposes. Whenever this assumption is not satisfied, neither policy can be very effective in controlling the economy, and they can create serious adverse consequences, as witnessed during the past few years.

Transitional Considerations

In all member countries of the Organization for Economic Cooperation and Development (OECD), government expenditures constitute between 25 percent and more than 50 percent of GNP. The public consensus seems to be established that this range of public expenditure is necessary for the well-being of the society. Accordingly in these countries the tax system, whatever form it takes, must collect revenues not too far from the same order of magnitude, and thus there is no question that decisions of individuals and firms cannot help but be influenced by the existing and prospective tax structure with which they must live. It is also true that some of these decisions are not reversible, and they define the environment in which many of the future decisions must be made for a long time to come. For these reasons, when the tax structure is changed unexpectedly and in significant ways, such changes can generate important transitional consequences that must be taken into account in designing reforms of the tax structure.

An example should make this point clearer. Suppose the U.S. tax system was revised so that the imputed rent on owner-occupied houses is no longer excluded from the tax base, and this new structure is in place for some time so that everyone has adjusted housing and other decisions accordingly. From an economic viewpoint the new pattern of the allocation of resources can be considered better than the old, and most experts would agree that equity is also better served; however, current housing values are based on the current tax treatment of the imputed rent of the owner-occupied houses, and once the exclusion of the imputed rent from the tax base is no longer possible, it is probable that the demand for housing services would decline substantially, and the market rate of existing houses would also decline markedly. Thus current home owners are likely to suffer considerable capital losses in the value of their houses in addition to the prospect of having to pay substantial increases in the carrying cost of houses after taxes. This effect may cause serious hardships for some owners, a fact that must be taken into account in designing the reform of the tax treatment of owner-occupied houses.

Tax Expenditures, Nontaxed Imputed Income, and Related Issues

The Magnitudes

The Congressional Budget Act defines tax expenditures as "those revenue losses attributable to provisions of the Federal tax laws which allow a special exclusion, exemption or deduction from gross income or which provide a special credit, a preferential rate of tax or a deferral of tax liability." The difficulty in applying this definition is specifying what is the base of the federal tax laws from which deviations will be measured. For example, the staff of the Joint Committee on Taxation does not consider the reduction in revenues from the zero bracket provision a tax expenditure but does consider the deduction for two-earner married couples a tax expenditure. The administration, in contrast, views the two-earner married couple tax deduction as part of the basic tax code. Recognizing this ambiguity, the staff of the joint committee has generally included as tax expenditures any item that some observers might conclude was a deviation from normal taxes. Also as a result of this ambiguity, lists of tax expenditures prepared by different parts of the government can differ.

The purposes of tax expenditures presumably are to encourage specific activities or to make the tax structure more equitable. There are, however, undoubtedly tax expenditures introduced into the tax code purely because of the political clout of a special interest group. Other tax expenditures may have been included in the tax code with good intentions, but the way in which they were implemented did not achieve their purpose. Even if a tax expenditure achieved its purpose, there may be alternative less costly ways to achieve the same purpose. (It is beyond the scope of this book to document the original purpose of every tax expenditure and to evaluate the success of the tax expenditure in achieving that purpose.)

According to the joint committee forecasts, there will be twenty tax expenditures in the individual tax code that individually will exceed $3.5 billion in fiscal 1988. These twenty items total $359.7 billion and represent 89 percent of the total of all individual tax expenditures for 1988 (table 3.2). Of importance in judging the political difficulty in changing these provisions, some of these twenty items provide tax relief to large groups of the population. Some of these tax expenditures provide substantial benefits to middle- and lower-income families, while others apply especially to upper-income families.

The total tax expenditures for corporations and individuals in fiscal 1983 are $295.3 billion, 81 percent of which flow to individuals (table 3.3). By fiscal 1988 total tax expenditures are projected to be $490.9 billion, an annual rate

Table 3.2

The twenty largest individual tax expenditures items, fiscal
1988 (millions)

Item	Amount
Net exclusion of pension contributions and earnings (employer plans)	$109,035
Deductibility of nonbusiness state and local government taxes other than on owner-occupied homes	39,010
Deductibility of mortgage interest on owner-occupied housing	37,950
Exclusion of employer contributions for medical insurance premiums and medical care	35,975
Exclusion of social security benefits for retired workers	23,045
Capital gains other than agriculture, timber, iron ore, and coal	18,820
Deductibility of property tax on owner-occupied homes	14,980
Deductibility of nonmortgage interest in excess of investment income	11,645
Exclusion of interest on life insurance savings	8,675
Deduction for two-earner married couples	8,460
Deductibility of charitable contributions, other than education and health	8,370
Deferral of capital gains on home sales	7,030
Exclusion of interest on general-purpose state and local government debt	5,580
Individual retirement plans	5,360
Exclusion of social security benefits for dependents and survivors	4,920
Investment credit, other than ESOPs, rehabilitation of structures, reforestation, and leasing	4,595
Capital gains at death	4,490
Deductibility of medical expenses	4,165
Net interest exclusion	3,945
Exclusion of workmen's compensation benefits	3,645
Total	359,695

Source: Estimates of Federal Tax Expenditures for Fiscal Years 1983–1988,
Joint Committee on Taxation, Washington, D.C., 1983.

Table 3.3
Sum of expenditure items, by type of taxpayer, fiscal years 1983–1988

	Corporations and Individuals	Corporations	Individuals
1983	$295,280	$56,225	$239,055
1984	327,455	67,915	259,540
1985	369,330	77,475	291,855
1986	411,575	83,210	328,365
1987	446,725	84,600	362,125
1988	490,850	86,495	404,355

Source: Joint Committee on Taxation, *Estimates of Federal Tax Expenditures for Fiscal Years 1983–1988* (Washington, D.C.: Government Printing Office, 1983).
Note: The totals represent the mathematical sum of the estimated fiscal year effect of each of the tax expenditure items included in the table.

of increase of 10.7 percent. Tables 3.4 and 3.5 contain a detailed summary of tax expenditures by function for 1983 through 1988 for individuals and corporations.

Omitted from these tables is the reduction in federal revenues from the exclusion of imputed income from reported income. This source of tax reduction usually is not considered a tax expenditure, although logically it probably should be despite the technical difficulties of measuring imputed income. The most important types of imputed income are the imputed rent of owner-occupied housing and the imputed rent of consumer durables. In calendar 1982 the national income accounts estimate the imputed rent of owner-occupied housing at $229.1 billion. At a 30 percent marginal tax rate, this sum, if taxed, would increase federal revenues by $68.7 billion. However, if imputed rent on owner-occupied housing itself were taxed, mortgage interest and property tax on owner-occupied housing would be normal business expenses and no longer would be considered tax expenditures. In addition owners would be able to deduct management cost, depreciation, and normal repairs. Since the deductibility of mortgage interest and property tax on owner-occupied housing is already included as a tax expenditure and owners cannot deduct depreciation or expenses associated with their homes, the inclusion of imputed rent as a tax expenditure item would not change the total of individual tax expenditures by nearly as much as the gross figures would suggest.

Treatment of Capital Gains

The treatment of capital gains has been one of the most controversial issues in taxation since the inception of the federal income tax. In the past capital gains have been treated as ordinary income on occasion and subject to preferential tax rates at other times, the degree of preferential treatment varying widely over different periods. The treatment of capital losses has also varied greatly in different years, ranging from no allowance for such losses to limited and full deductibility from capital gains or other income. Long-term and short-term capital gains also have been treated differently for tax purposes, with the specific provisions subject to substantial changes from time to time. In particular, provisions relating to the holding period distinguishing short-term from long-term capital gains have significantly varied.

Currently for assets held longer than six months, 40 percent of realized net gains are included in adjusted gross revenues for tax purposes, while 50 percent of losses from shorter-term transactions are deductible from taxable income. Only realized gains are subject to taxation, and capital gains taxes can be completely avoided if the assets are held until the owner's death. As a result the effective rate of capital gains taxation is very much smaller than the normal rate on realized gains. Thus for several years in the

Table 3.4
Tax expenditure estimates for individuals, by function for fiscal years (millions)

Function	1983	1984	1985	1986	1987	1988
National Defense						
Exclusion of benefits and allowances to armed forces personnel	$ 2,205	$ 2,250	$ 2,380	$ 2,520	$ 2,670	$ 2,820
Exclusion of military disability pensions	165	160	165	175	185	195
International Affairs						
Exclusion of income earned abroad by U.S. citizens	1,285	1,300	1,365	1,435	1,505	1,580
General Science, Space, and Technology						
Expensing of research and development expenditures	105	120	125	125	130	135
Credit for increasing research activities	30	35	40	30	5	a
Energy						
Expensing of exploration and developing costs						
Oil and gas	875	800	815	855	900	950
Excess of percentage over cost depletion						
Oil and gas	1,425	1,275	1,305	1,410	1,505	1,625
Other fuels	15	15	15	15	15	20
Capital gains treatment of royalties from coal	140	145	160	175	190	205

	5	10	15	20	20	25
Exclusion of interest on state and local government industrial development bonds for energy production facilities	5	10	15	20	20	25
Residential energy credits						
Supply incentives	340	450	610	700	70	
Conservation incentives	330	305	305	260		
Alternative, conservation, and new technology credits						
Supply incentives	10	10	5			
Conservation incentives	[a]	[a]	[a]			
Natural Resources and Environment						
Expensing of exploration and development costs, nonfuel minerals	[a]	[a]	[a]	[a]	[a]	[a]
Excess of percentage over cost depletion, nonfuel minerals	10	10	15	15	15	15
Capital gains treatment of certain timber income	95	125	150	175	205	230
Investment credit and seven-year amortization for reforestation expenditures	10	10	10	10	10	10
Capital gains treatment of iron ore	5	5	5	5	5	10
Exclusion of interest on state and local government pollution control bonds	440	505	565	620	680	745

Table 3.4 (*continued*)

Function	1983	1984	1985	1986	1987	1988
Tax incentives for preservation of historic structures	130	165	215	275	355	460
Agriculture						
Expensing of certain capital outlays	475	495	510	530	545	565
Capital gains treatment of certain income	455	475	500	530	545	565
Deductibility of patronage dividends and certain other items of cooperatives	−390	−400	−410	−425	−435	−450
Exclusion of certain cost-sharing payments	50	45	40	30	25	25
Commerce and Housing						
Dividend exclusion	445	435	440	450	460	480
Reinvestment of dividends in stock of public utilities	365	415	450	230		
Net interest exclusion			1,110	3,095	3,480	3,945
Exclusion of state and local government industrial development bonds	570	675	800	985	1,180	1,310
Exclusion of interest on certain savings certificates	2,355	550				
Exclusion of interest on life insurance savings	4,805	5,170	5,805	6,640	7,590	8,675

Deductibility of nonmortgage interest in excess of investment income	7,735	8,160	8,815	9,590	10,550	11,645
Deductibility of mortgage interest on owner-occupied homes	25,065	27,945	30,130	32,785	35,305	37,950
Deductibility of property tax on owner-occupied homes	8,765	9,535	10,480	11,710	13,215	14,980
Exclusion of interest on state and local government housing bonds for owner-occupied housing	450	485	475	445	415	385
Exclusion of interest on state and local government housing bonds for rental housing	285	355	430	510	585	665
Deferral of capital gains on home sales	3,770	4,895	5,625	6,000	6,480	7,030
Exclusion of capital gains on home sales for persons age 55 and over	1,255	1,630	1,875	2,000	2,160	2,345
Depreciation on rental housing in excess of straight line	575	665	720	760	795	820
Depreciation on buildings other than rental housing in excess of straight line	150	165	185	210	230	250
Accelerated depreciation on equipment other than leased property	1,015	2,460	2,845	2,825	2,255	1,915
Amortization of business start-up costs	105	160	230	285	315	355
Capital gains other than agriculture, timber, iron ore, and coal	14,955	14,320	15,365	16,440	17,590	18,820
Capital gains at death	3,975	3,565	3,665	3,920	4,195	4,490

Table 3.4 (continued)

Function	1983	1984	1985	1986	1987	1988
Investment credit, other than ESOPs, rehabilitation of structures, reforestation, and leasing	3,220	3,350	3,615	3,945	4,245	4,595
Transportation						
Amortization of motor carrier operating rights	5	5	5	5	a	
Exclusion of interest on state and local government mass transit bonds	15	25	20	15	10	20
Community and Regional Development						
Five-year amortization for housing rehabilitation	30	35	35	35	35	35
Investment credit for rehabilitation of structures other than historic structures	160	165	160	165	180	200
Education, Training, Employment, and Social Services						
Exclusion of scholarship and fellowship income	415	375	395	410	435	460
Exclusion of interest on state and local government student loan bonds	70	100	125	155	190	225
Parental personal exemption for students age 19 and over	995	950	885	895	905	920

Exclusion of employee meals and lodging (other than military)	680	725	795	870	945	1,030
Employer educational assistance	40	20				
Exclusion of contributions to prepaid legal services plans	25	25	10			
Exclusion for employer-provided child care	10	25	55	85	120	155
Deductibility of charitable contributions (education)	495	495	580	735	660	615
Deductibility of charitable contributions, other than education and health	6,795	6,765	7,930	10,030	9,030	8,370
Credit for child and dependent care expenses	1,520	1,765	2,190	2,465	2,765	3,160
Targeted jobs credit	75	70	30	[a]		
Deduction for two-earner married couples	3,555	5,835	6,350	6,935	7,600	8,460
Deduction for adoption expenses	10	10	10	10	15	15
Health						
Exclusion of employer contributions for medical insurance premiums and medical care	18,645	21,300	24,280	27,680	31,555	35,975
Deductibility of medical expenses	3,105	2,630	3,070	3,370	3,740	4,165
Exclusion of interest on state and local government hospital bonds	385	470	545	625	700	780
Deductibility of charitable contributions (health)	995	990	1,160	1,470	1,320	1,225

Table 3.4 (*continued*)

Function	1983	1984	1985	1986	1987	1988
Income Security						
Exclusion of social security benefits						
Disability insurance benefits	1,690	1,660	1,695	1,755	1,840	1,930
OASI benefits for retired workers	15,685	16,680	18,070	19,640	21,275	23,045
Benefits for dependents and survivors	3,765	3,870	4,095	4,355	4,630	4,920
Exclusion of railroad retirement system benefits	780	765	765	745	755	775
Exclusion of workmen's compensation benefits	1,870	2,090	2,395	2,755	3,170	3,645
Exclusion of special benefits for disabled coal miners	170	165	165	160	160	165
Exclusion of untaxed unemployment insurance benefits	3,260	3,020	2,585	2,405	2,265	2,120
Exclusion of public assistance benefits	430	430	440	455	470	485
Exclusion of disability pay	145	135	130	130	130	130
Net exclusion of pension contributions and earnings						
Employer plans	49,700	56,560	66,365	78,310	92,405	109,035
Plans for self-employed	1,065	1,050	1,070	1,115	1,165	1,220
Individual retirement plans	2,695	3,180	3,705	4,240	4,745	5,360
Exclusion of other employee benefits						
Premiums on group-term life insurance	2,100	2,250	2,465	2,715	2,985	3,285
Premiums on accident and disability insurance	115	120	125	130	135	140
Additional exemption for the blind	35	35	35	35	35	35
Additional exemption for the elderly	2,365	2,410	2,570	2,720	2,410	3,130

Tax credit for the elderly	135	135	135	135	135	135
Deductibility of casualty and theft losses	575	380	470	520	590	670
Earned income credit[b]	385	330	290	215	155	210
Veteran Benefits and Services						
Exclusion of veterans' disability compensation	1,820	1,830	1,950	1,995	2,070	2,145
Exclusion of veterans' pensions	310	290	280	275	275	275
Exclusion of GI bill benefits	130	130	115	100	90	65
General Government						
Credits and deductions for political contributions	190	200	220	220	230	240
General Purpose Fiscal Assistance						
Exclusion of interest on general purpose state and local government debt	3,435	3,870	4,295	4,715	5,130	5,580
Deductibility of nonbusiness state and local government taxes other than on owner-occupied homes	20,060	21,770	26,605	29,970	34,125	39,010
Interest						
Deferral of interest on savings bonds	50	160	225	290	355	410

Source: Joint Committee on Taxation, *Estimates of Federal Tax Expenditures for Fiscal Years 1983–1988* (Washington, D.C.: Government Printing Office, 1983).

Note: All estimates are based on the tax law enacted through the Ninety-seventh Congress.

a. Less than $2.5 million. All estimates have been rounded to the nearest $5 million.

b. The figures in the table indicate the effect of the earned income credit on receipts. The increases in outlays are: $1,197 million in 1983, $1,119 million in 1984, $1,032 million in 1985, $1,004 million in 1986, $968 million in 1987, and $910 million in 1988.

Table 3.5
Tax expenditure estimates for corporations by function, fiscal years (millions)

Function	1983	1984	1985	1986	1987	1988
International Affairs						
Deferral of income of domestic international sales corporations	$1,390	$ 1,185	$ 1,075	$ 1,050	$ 1,075	$ 1,110
Deferral of income of controlled foreign corporations	430	345	375	390	420	455
General Science, Space, and Technology						
Expensing of research and development expenditures	2,165	2,370	2,360	2,425	2,485	2,535
Credit for increasing research activities	615	650	660	305	65	25
Suspension of regulations relating to allocation under section 861 of research and experimental expenditures	120	60	[a]			
Energy						
Expensing of exploration and developing costs						
Oil and gas	660	440	590	740	835	895
Other fuels	30	30	35	35	40	40
Excess of percentage over cost depletion						
Oil and gas	375	430	445	465	510	555
Other fuels	325	350	355	380	410	440
Capital gains treatment of royalties from coal	35	40	40	45	50	55
Alternative fuel production credit	5	20	25	40	105	285

Alcohol fuel credit[b]	5	5	5	5	5	5
Exclusion of interest on state and local government industrial development bonds for energy production facilities	15	20	30	40	55	70
Alternative, conservation, and new technology credits						
Supply incentives	215	200	175	100	35	20
Conservation incentives	135	35	15	5	[a]	
Energy credit for intercity buses	5	5	5	[a]		
Natural Resources and Environment						
Expensing of exploration and development costs, nonfuel minerals	55	60	65	75	80	85
Excess of percentage over cost depletion, nonfuel minerals	270	295	310	335	355	380
Capital gains treatment of certain timber income	275	390	430	500	575	595
Investment credit and seven-year amortization for reforestation expenditures	[a]	[a]	[a]	[a]	[a]	[a]
Capital gains treatment of iron ore	5	5	5	5	5	10
Exclusion of interest on state and local government pollution control bonds	900	1,025	1,140	1,255	1,375	1,510
Exclusion of payments in aid of construction of water, sewage, gas, and electric utilities	45	75	75	80	75	70
Tax incentives for preservation of historic structures	65	90	110	140	185	240

Table 3.5 (*continued*)

Function	1983	1984	1985	1986	1987	1988
Agriculture						
Expensing of certain capital outlays	85	90	95	100	100	105
Capital gains treatment of certain income	30	35	35	40	40	45
Deductibility of patronage dividends and certain other items of cooperatives	950	980	1,010	1,040	1,075	1,110
Commerce and Housing						
Exclusion of state and local government industrial development bonds	2,355	2,790	3,265	3,875	4,385	4,615
Exemption of credit union income	170	185	200	220	240	260
Excess bad debt reserves of financial institutions	335	575	785	930	1,060	1,030
Exclusion of interest on state and local government housing bonds for owner-occupied housing	1,060	1,190	1,190	1,145	1,105	1,070
Exclusion of interest on state and local government housing bonds for rental housing	585	735	880	1,035	1,185	1,345
Depreciation on rental housing in excess of straight line	120	155	165	170	180	185
Depreciation on buildings other than rental housing in excess of straight line	175	200	215	240	265	295

Accelerated depreciation on equipment other than leased property	9,510	15,865	18,860	17,445	14,110	13,890
Safe harbor leasing						
Accelerated depreciation and deferral	1,745	1,885	1,635	1,285	1,040	525
Investment credit	1,625	915	705	710	515	280
Amortization of business start-up costs	15	20	25	30	35	40
Capital gains other than agriculture, timber, iron ore, and coal	1,770	2,075	2,130	2,305	2,475	2,695
Reduced rates on the first $100,000 of corporate income	5,690	6,525	7,025	8,060	8,765	9,090
Investment credit, other than ESOPs, rehabilitation of structures, reforestation, and leasing	9,965	12,315	16,075	19,870	21,650	22,860
Transportation						
Amortization of motor carrier operating rights	70	70	50	15	5	a
Deferral of tax on shipping companies	30	40	40	45	45	45
Exclusion of interest on state and local government mass transit bonds	45	65	75	75	65	75
Community and Regional Development						
Five-year amortization for housing rehabilitation	20	25	25	25	25	25
Investment credit for rehabilitation of structures other than historic structures	175	200	185	195	215	235
Education, Training, Employment, and Social Services						
Exclusion of interest on state and local government student loan bonds	150	200	260	320	390	460

Table 3.5 (*continued*)

Function	1983	1984	1985	1986	1987	1988
Tax credit for ESOPs	1,250	1,375	1,875	2,235	2,330	950
Deductibility of charitable contributions (education)	280	345	360	415	480	525
Deductibility of charitable contributions, other than education and health	350	425	445	515	590	645
Targeted jobs credit	215	395	355	155	30	5
Health						
Exclusion of interest on state and local government hospital bonds	795	960	1,115	1,265	1,420	1,580
Deductibility of charitable contributions (health)	175	215	225	255	295	325
Tax credit for orphan drug research	10	15	15	10		
General Purpose Fiscal Assistance						
Exclusion of interest on general purpose state and local government debt	6,985	7,850	8,695	9,530	10,370	11,280
Tax credit for corporations receiving income from doing business in U.S. possessions	1,350	1,075	1,135	1,240	1,375	1,525

Source: Joint Committee on Taxation, *Estimates of Federal Tax Expenditures for Fiscal Years 1983–1988* (Washington, D.C.: Government Printing Office, 1983).

Note: All estimates are based on the tax law enacted through the Ninety-seventh Congress.

a. Less than $2.5 million. All estimates have been rounded to the nearest $5 million.

b. In addition, the exemption from the excise tax for alcohol fuels results in a reduction in excise tax receipts, net of the income tax effect, of approximately $40 million for 1983, $60 million for 1984, $80 million for 1985, $95 million for 1986, and $110 million for 1987 and 1988.

past the effective capital gains tax is estimated to have been only about 5 percent.[27]

As distinguished from their treatment in taxable income, all real capital gains, which consist of net gains adjusted for inflation, would be considered part of economic income. This would be true for unrealized as well as realized gains. In the presence of inflationary price movements, nominal capital gains must be adjusted downward (and may be negative) since only the value (in current dollars) of the change in real assets should be included in income. The effective tax rate on capital gains as a whole is, in most periods and for most taxpayers, substantially less than it would be if all real capital gains, both realized and unrealized, were included in taxable as well as in economic income. This is not necessarily true in periods of rampant inflation when owners of financial assets, including equities and debt, may suffer large real losses; however, the likelihood of sizable losses on common stocks resulting from unexpected inflation has been substantially reduced by changes in corporate taxation in recent years.[28]

Many reasons have been advanced for the preferential tax treatment of capital gains. Perhaps most important it is widely believed that the more favorable this treatment, the better for saving and investment.[29] From this point of view private saving is supposed to be stimulated by the higher after-tax rate of return brought on by lower taxes on all forms of capital income, while the effective cost of capital to all forms of investment is lowered. There is, however, no strong theoretical or empirical reason for believing that a decline in personal income taxes will have a substantial, sustained effect on the propensity to save or on the cost of capital. Although there are strong theoretical and empirical grounds for expecting the cost of capital to be positively related to the level of corporate income taxes so that a reduction in such taxes would probably stimulate investment, the long-run effect on capital formation is likely to be moderate if the after-tax interest elasticity of saving is as low as the evidence suggests.[30] Moreover, for a given over-all level of taxation, any favorable effects on capital formation of lower marginal tax rates on capital income would be counterbalanced by unfavorable effects on labor incentives of higher taxation of labor income.

So far we have considered taxation of real capital gains to be approximately equivalent in their impact on capital formation to the same amount of taxes on any other form of capital income. This is not necessarily true theoretically in view of the greater uncertainty associated with capital gains than with ordinary income and the much more asymmetric impact of capital gains taxation.[31] Empirically the evidence on the impact of the level of capital gains taxation on capital values (and hence on the cost of capital) is quite scanty and not at all conclusive. Thus for common stocks, which have been subject to more analysis of price effects of capital gains taxation than other capital assets, some time-series analyses indicate a significant negative effect of capital gains taxation, but the evidence is quite weak and inconsistent.[32] The problem with time-series analysis is the difficulty in using the small number of changes in the relevant tax laws to explain the extremely volatile movements in stock prices. Basically the case for a substantial impact of capital gains taxation on stock prices has yet to be proved or refuted, but there is no strong reason for believing that the effect of such taxes on stock prices is markedly different from that for other forms of capital income taxation.

A second important reason advanced for the preferential tax treatment of at least unrealized capital gains, normally a much larger component of the total than the realized gains, is the great difficulty in measuring a high proportion of unrealized gains and in financing the tax payments that would be associated with these gains without forcing undesirable and costly asset liquidation. Such problems are generally unimportant for readily marketable securities but are extremely large for nonmarketable securities and owned homes, two other major forms of assets held by individual taxpayers. For all assets, including marketable securities, the desirability of adjusting nominal capital gains in a period of marked inflation introduces a further complication.

There is one other respect in which capital gains taxation is frequently claimed to have an adverse effect on financial markets and economic efficiency: by depressing market liquidity. The theoretical rationale for this claim is that since capital gains taxes can be substantially reduced by holding the assets for a period in excess of six months and can be avoided altogether if carried over into the taxpayer's estate, a taxpayer has a strong financial incentive to hold the asset for at least six months, even if nontax economic considerations would lead that person to switch funds into more attractive investments. Such a constraint on these investments presumably would lead to a less efficient allocation of economic resources, though it is extremely difficult to determine the magnitude of the effect and even more difficult to assess its economic importance.[33]

A substantial amount of empirical analysis has been devoted to the effect of the holding period provisions in the tax laws on the timing and amount of capital gains realizations and on the implications for tax revenues collected, but the results are again inconclusive.[34] Virtually all show a significant positive effect of liberalized holding period provisions (permitting the more favorable taxation of long-term capital gains to apply to shorter-term holding periods) on accelerating realizations; however, they differ widely on the size of the effect and on whether the greater realizations are sufficient to offset the lower levels of effective tax rates or whether the level of increased realizations found at the time of capital gains tax changes is likely to carry over to longer periods of time.[35] Our evaluation of these different studies is that it appears that capital gains taxes do inhibit realizations, thus probably introducing some allocational inefficiencies, but it is not clear that the effect is large in the long run, very important in the short run, or sufficient to offset the loss in tax revenues associated with lower tax rates.

While this discussion raises some questions about the extent of the alleged inefficiencies introduced by capital gains taxation, such taxation does introduce a number of serious problems not associated with the taxation of ordinary income. If taxation is shifted from an income to a consumption base, the problem of appropriate capital gains taxation would disappear in the long run but only at the expense of some major transitional difficulties; moreover, even in the long run, the elimination or minimization of capital gains taxation would, other things equal, result in a less progressive tax structure.

Gift and Inheritance Taxes

A proper concern for any government like the United States is the distribution of wealth among its citizens. The distribution of wealth has implications for both equity and efficiency. Extreme concentration of wealth in the hands of a limited number of families may lead to an excessive concentration of economic and political power. Such power would allow these types of families to force their will on society in ways that would not have been possible without their wealth.

There is a long tradition in the United States that such concentrations of power should be avoided. Underlying the antitrust laws, for example, is the philosophical principle that no corporation should have sufficient monopolistic power to charge a price different from the competitive price. As another example, the Constitution gives each state two senators for the express purpose of reducing the concentration of power in the more populated states.

A major ideal of a democratic society is that two individuals with similar physical and intellectual capabilities should have the same opportunities to realize these capabilities. It should not make a difference who their parents were. Not only does this goal seem fair and equitable, it also will lead to greater efficiency in the allocation and use of scarce resources. Finally, some believe that it is inequitable for one child to receive a large inheritance, just by accident of birth, while another similar child lives in poverty, also just by accident of birth.

A democratic government must also permit individuals to accumulate wealth and some rights to bequeath this wealth so as to encourage the entrepreneurial spirit necessary for a competitive society. Counterbalancing this need are the proper concerns of the government to maintain equity among its citizens and to avoid extreme concentrations of economic and political power. Where the line should be drawn is ultimately a political decision.

The primary tools available to federal and state governments to affect the distribution of wealth are graduated taxes on investment and other income and estate and gift taxes.[36] These two types of taxes, one on current income and the other on gifts and bequests, together shape the distribution of wealth among individuals or households.[37]

In any reform of the tax system the tax codes for current income and for gifts and bequests should be considered as a unit. If the tax on investment and other income is reduced, some individuals undoubtedly will accumulate more wealth during their lifetime than they otherwise would have. If it is desired to make the tax change neutral with respect to the distribution of wealth, estate taxes would have to be adjusted appropriately. The corollary of this statement is that any reform of the personal income tax in the direction of a consumption tax should carefully evaluate the adequacy of the current gift and estate taxes in the perspective of the goals of society.

Any changes in the federal gift and estate tax would begin with the current tax schedule, which includes gifts made over a person's lifetime as part of the final bequest but in a complicated way and further allows nontaxable transfers of assets between husband and wife. In 1987 an unmarried person having made no gifts during his or her lifetime would be able to bequeath an estate of up to $600,000 with no federal tax. Any amount in excess of $600,000 would be taxed at a minimum rate of 37 percent. The maximum marginal rate is 50 percent, which is applicable to those sums in an estate in excess of $3.1 million.[38] Thus, in 1987, the average federal tax rate on an estate of $1 million with no prior gifts would be 16.4 percent, on an estate of $5 million 44.0 percent, on an estate of $10 million 47.0 percent, and on an estate of $100 million 49.7 percent.[39]

4 Individual Income Taxes

Among the principles that should guide the design of a tax system are horizontal equity, vertical equity, economic efficiency, simplicity, and administrative ease. In applying these principles, there are substantial elements of subjective judgment in defining vertical equity and in working out practical compromises acceptable to a large majority of the public when two or more of these principles conflict.

The basic federal income tax code of the United States currently in effect was designed in 1954. It was an impressive achievement, but as with any other large, complex legislation, public and political leaders subsequently found some of its provisions to be undesirable. In addition, whenever society as a whole felt that public support for some specific activities was necessary, modifying the tax code to accommodate such needs was often more expedient than appropriating specific expenditures for them. Finally, a large number of interest groups have been able to persuade political leaders to introduce special provisions into the code. Most of these are relatively small items when considered separately and hence have aroused little opposition from the general public. But when they are taken together, these small provisions have reduced the tax base by significant amounts.

Evolution of the Tax Code

The 1954 code was quite progressive in its incidence on different economic groups, and in particular the marginal rates for upper-income brackets were quite high, perhaps excessively so. As the level of income per capita rose in the United States, the revenue from income taxes rose considerably faster, due to this progressivity. Tax revisions undertaken between 1963 and 1965 were designed to take advantage of this situation and to reduce marginal rates while maintaining federal revenue at a level consistent with the full employment balanced budget.[1]

Between 1955 and 1981 the size of the personal exemption as a proportion of per capita personal income declined dramatically, while the availability of special provisions for exclusion of certain types of income and deduction of a number of items from the tax base increased.[2] The former tends to make the taxable income a larger proportion of personal income (as defined in the national income and product accounts), while the latter makes it a smaller proportion. The net result is that aggregate taxable income, as a proportion of personal income, increased slowly but steadily from 1955 to 1970 and remained reasonably constant thereafter.[3]

It would be very helpful to separate the net effects into the gross effect of the proportional decline in personal exemption on the one hand and the gross effect of increased availability of exclusion and deduction provisions on the other. Unfortunately, precise separation is impossible; table 4.1 provides only a very approximate order of magnitude of the effects.

The calculations in table 4.1 ignore the impact of the standard deduction on the assumption that this deduction is roughly the same proportion of per capita personal income in 1981 as in 1955.[4] From table 4.1 actual taxable income in 1955 was roughly 62 percent of the personal income after exemptions; if the personal exemption in 1981 were the same proportion of per capita income as in 1955, the comparable figure in 1981 would have been 50 percent.[5] This trend indicates a clear reduction in the potential tax base defined in this way as between these two years. The net effect was that the reduction in personal exemptions and the increase in provisions for various deductions and exclusions (which higher-income groups are better able to utilize than lower-income groups) tended to make the individual income tax system less progressive.

Meanwhile although the apparent progressivity of the marginal rate structure has been reduced, the general increase in per capita income over the years (due to both increases in real income and general inflation) pushed more and more individuals into higher tax brackets, especially for the middle-income ranges, thus tending to make the system more progressive. The net result was that the progressivity of the individual income tax system remained roughly constant until around 1975 and then declined. Detailed data on actual distribution of the tax burden among income groups after 1981 are not yet available, but the general indication is that the progressivity of the tax system has been further reduced by recent changes in the tax code.

Complex deduction and exclusion provisions that apply unevenly to different taxpayers produce significant and frequent violations of horizontal equity. For higher-income groups and to a lesser extent for middle-income taxpayers, marginal tax rates are much higher than average rates, creating some economic inefficiency. These conditions have contributed to a general sense of public dissatisfaction with the federal income tax system. Expert observers also have felt that the tax code no longer adheres to the basic guiding principles. The revision of the tax code of

Table 4.1
Gross effects of deduction and exclusion provisions other than personal exemptions on the tax base, 1955, 1980, 1981

	1955	1980	1981
(1) Personal income (billions of dollars)	310.1	2,165.3	2,435.0
(2) Average per capita exemption (dollars)	653.0	1,110.0	1,110.0
(3) Population (millions)	165.3	227.1	229.5
(4) Personal income per capita ((1)/(3))	1,876.0	9,538.0	10,592.0
(5) Taxable income (billions of dollars)	128.0	1,252.0	1,383.7
(6) Per capita exemption using the 1955 proportion ((4) × (653/1,876))	653.0	3,319.0	3,686.0
(7) Total exemption using the 1955 proportion ((6) × (3))	107.2	753.7	845.9
(8) Personal income-exemption (1955 Basis) ((1) − (7))	202.9	1,411.6	1,589.1
(9) Total exemption using the current exemption ((2) × (3))	107.2	252.1	254.7
(10) Increase in taxable income due to less than proportionate increase in per capita exemption ((7) − (9))	0.0	501.6	591.2
(11) Taxable income if the per capita exemption remained the same proportion of per capita personal income, and other deductions and exclusions were those in effect historically ((5) − (10))	128.0	750.4	792.5
(12) Reduction of tax base due to deduction and exclusion provisions ((8) − (11))	74.9	661.2	796.6
(13) (11)/(8)	0.62	0.53	0.5

Note: We start from personal income as defined by national income account, row 1. Row 4 shows the pattern of personal income per capita, and row 6 then shows what personal exemption per capita would have been had it remained proportional to personal income per capita for these three years. Row 7 indicates aggregate exemptions if per capita exemption were as shown in row 6, and row 8 reports the potential maximum tax base after personal exemption. Row 9 is the actual historical values of aggregate personal exemptions taken, and therefore row 10 shows how much more aggregate personal exemption would have been if per capita exemption were as shown in row 6 rather than its actual historical value. Row 11, obtained by subtracting row 10 from actual historical taxable income,

1981, while reducing the marginal tax rates for all taxpayers, did not address itself to the issue of the basic defects of the tax structure accumulated over the years.

Progressive versus Flat Rate Structure: Some Elementary Considerations

It is useful to note how certain provisions contribute to or detract from the progressivity of an income tax system, as measured by the relationship of the average tax rate to the level of income. For the purpose of the discussion, we assume that the definition of total income is given and, specifically, that gross income is clearly defined and no itemized deductions are allowed.[6]

First, other things equal, the more progressive is the marginal tax rate structure, the more progressive is the tax system in terms of the average rate of tax.

Second, most income tax systems define some basic amounts of income that are exempt from taxation, such as personal exemptions and standard deductions. They can be given in two forms. The first is to give as personal exemptions and standard deductions a fixed amount that

---

therefore is an indication of what the tax base would have been if the personal exemption per capita were as given in row 6 while all other deduction and exclusion provisions were those in effect historically. To put it another way, row 12, obtained by subtracting row 11 from row 8, indicates the amount of reduction of the tax base due to deduction and exclusion provisions from the potential maximum tax base after personal exemption. Row 13, the ratio of row 11 to row 8, merely indicates the proportion of the potential maximum tax base represented by the remaining tax base, under the assumption that the per capita exemption is held at the same proportion of per capita personal income as in 1955. That is, 1 minus the ratio shown in row 13 is the proportional measure of the tax erosion. This analysis depends on the reasonable assumption that personal exemptions and other deductions and exclusions rarely overlap, so that they can be considered additive for practical purposes.

is independent of the level of the taxpayer's income, as provided for under the current U.S. tax code. Taxpayers are asked first to compute the gross income, subtract the amount of deductions allowed, and then apply the tax table to the amount after the deduction. The second is to give credits against gross taxes. Taxpayers are asked first to compute the gross income, apply the tax table directly to the gross income, and then to reduce the gross tax liability so computed by the amount of the credit. In this case the amount of the credit does not vary with the level of the taxpayer's income. It is then easy to show that for a given amount of total revenue loss to the Treasury and a given schedule of marginal tax rates, a basic credit against the gross tax liability makes the tax system more progressive than does a basic deduction.[7] The only exception to this rule occurs when the marginal tax rate is constant throughout all levels of taxable income so that the two systems lead to an identical result.

Third, given the marginal tax rate schedule and the decision of whether to provide a basic deduction or a basic credit against gross tax liability, the larger is the deduction or credit, the more progressive is the system.

The current federal individual income tax system has a substantially progressive marginal tax rate structure even after the 1981 revision of the code. Some economists and politicians are currently suggesting a flat rate schedule designed so as to produce the same revenues. Such a tax schedule would reduce the progressivity of the overall tax system and probably would make it regressive. To offset this loss of progressivity, such proposals usually call for an increase in the basic deductions (personal exemptions and standard deductions) and sometimes the conversion of these deductions into tax credits against gross liabilities. This type of proposal would indeed preserve the progressivity of the tax system near the lower end of the income range, but this measure alone, together with a flat rate schedule, must necessarily shift the tax burden from higher-income groups to middle-income groups.[8]

It is not possible to maintain the current level of progressivity with a flat tax, even with large standard deductions or tax credit.[9] Replacing deductions with tax credits is more effective in preserving progressivity. Even so any tax program that maintains the same degree of progressivity and the same level of total revenue as the current income tax rate schedule will require progressive marginal rates.

It is possible for individual taxpayers to have tax credits in excess of their gross tax liabilities. These excess credits can simply be ignored, leading to no transaction between the taxpayer and the Internal Revenue Service (IRS). Alternatively the tax code can recognize the excess credit and refund the net excess credit to the taxpayer. From the point of view of efficiency and equity, it seems preferable to make excess credits refundable and to replace most of the current transfer payment programs with such refundable credits—essentially a negative income tax. This, however, would lead to a fundamental reformulation of the social programs and transfer systems of the government, especially much of the social security system, and none of the proposals being considered currently contemplates such a sweeping change.[10]

By reducing the progressivity of the marginal rate schedule, it is almost inevitable that the tax burden will be shifted somewhat away from the low- and high-income groups toward the middle-income groups. Thus both to counter this tendency and maintain the level of total revenue available to the Treasury, the tax base must be broadened significantly, as proposed by a number of reform measures currently under discussion. Although base broadening in general would tend to increase the progressivity of the individual income tax system and thus counter the reduction of the progressivity due to the reduction of the marginal tax rates, available information does not permit a fully satisfactory estimate of the quantitative effects of the base-broadening measures that have been proposed. It is thus uncertain whether these base-broadening measures would be sufficient to offset completely the natural tendency of a flatter marginal tax rate structure to shift the burden of the tax toward the middle-income groups.

Virtually all proposals advanced recently for reforming the federal income tax system share some common features. All propose to eliminate many, if not all, of the deduction and exclusion provisions, thus broadening the tax base and reducing the opportunity for significantly violating horizontal equity. All propose to reduce marginal tax rates significantly over the entire range of income, especially at the upper levels. In order to offset the redistributional effects of a shift in the tax burden from the upper-income to the lower-income groups that would be generated by the proposed revision of marginal tax rates, these proposals provide for an increase in some combination of personal exemptions and standard deductions.

In terms of the set of principles already discussed, our simple analysis sugge~ 's a few basic features that any reform proposal must contain in order to reduce marginal tax rates and at the same time maintain the progressivity present in the current federal income tax system. First, it is probably not possible to design an income tax system with a strictly flat marginal rate. Such a system does not have enough flexibility to approximate the distributional effects of the current federal income tax system. Moreover it would almost inevitably reduce the tax burden of both low- and high-income groups at the expense of middle-income groups. Feasible alternatives are ones in which the marginal tax rate structure is progressive but less so than the current federal income tax system.

If the marginal tax rate structure is to be only mildly progressive, then the tax base must be broadened as completely as possible in order to achieve the following goals: generate the necessary revenues for the government, preserve the same degree of progressivity as in the current code, and ensure equal treatment of income from different sources for horizontal equity and economic efficiency.

In a system with a moderately progressive marginal tax rate structure, it is important that the low-income bracket in which the tax liability is zero or close to zero be of a reasonable width. Providing credits against the gross tax liability rather than deductions from the gross income will have the greatest impact on progressivity, everything else constant.

Finally, in such a system, it may not be feasible to include all income in the tax base, mostly because of the difficulty of measurement. The unrealized portion of capital gains is an obvious example of such a difficulty. To tax unrealized capital gains and other income that have not been taxed and to preserve a socially acceptable wealth distribution in the population, any reform of the income tax system should be coupled with a careful analysis of estate or gift taxes.[11]

With these points in mind, we proceed with a review of major tax expenditures (reduction of the tax base) contained in the current tax system and then to a discussion of the B-G reform proposal.

On Major Tax Expenditures

The current tax code contains a large number of provisions for deductions of specific items and exclusions of certain types of income. Many of these existed when the basic design of the tax code was put in place in 1954, but many more have been added to the code since 1954. One measure of the size of these special provisions is what is known as tax expenditures, a measure of the tax revenue lost due to these special provisions. The total tax expenditure due to these special deduction and exclusion provisions is estimated by the Joint Committee on Taxation and by the Congressional Budget Office to have been roughly $239.3 billion in 1983 in the individual income tax system and some $56.7 billion in the corporate profit tax system.

The most important of these tax expenditures in terms of the size of the revenue loss are listed in table 2.2. The complete list compiled by the Joint Comittee on Taxation, together with the committee's estimates of the revenue losses involved for 1983 and the proposed disposition of these items according to the proposal, is given in appendix A. The most comprehensive evaluation of each item, together with a suggested disposition, is provided in a Department of Treasury document, *Blueprints for Basic Tax Reform*.[12]

The basic thrust of the analysis in *Blueprints* is that virtually all of these tax expenditures should be eliminated, and most economists would probably agree with this assessment. It is, however, difficult to eliminate all of them primarily because some types of income are extremely difficult to measure, especially on a periodic basis such as every year. Unrealized capital gains are in this category, although they clearly constitute income as defined by economists. The total value of such gains is large enough so that their treatment for income tax purposes would have material impact on the total revenue from the federal individual income tax system and on distributional effects of the tax system.[13] *Blueprints* concludes that it is virtually impossible to include unrealized capital gains in the tax base and proposes that only realized capital gains, adjusted for the effects of the general price inflation, be included in the base. Many tax experts believe that this may be the only feasible tax treatment of capital gains.

Nonetheless unrealized capital gains ultimately should be recognized as income and be subject to taxation. There are some transactions under the current law in which unrealized capital gains escape taxation. Two important transactions in which unrealized gains are not currently taxed are the transference of assets at death and the gifts of assets, especially to charitable institutions. At death the gain should be recognized either as income for the deceased or in some other way through estate or inheritance taxes. For gifts economic and equity considerations would seem to dictate that the difference between the acquisition cost and the valuation of the gift should be imputed to the donor as income.

Another major difficulty arises when the nature of the transactions is unclear. An important example of this type of difficulty occurs in defining the relationship between the individual income tax system and the social security system, especially old age and survivor's insurance. If the social security system is indeed strictly an insurance system and the contributions by individuals are the actuarially fair premiums for the promised benefits, then it is clear how the social security system should be handled in the individual income tax system. Employee contributions should not be deducted from the tax base of employees (as they are not under the current system), and employer contributions should be imputed to the employees as income or included directly in the employer's tax base. The earnings of the social security funds might be imputed to the employees as income, but there is probably no practical way to impute such income. Finally, the benefits should not be taxed since they are simply an exchange between two types of assets already owned by individuals. There is, however, only a tenuous relationship between contributions to social insurance by individuals and their employers on the one hand and benefits that individuals receive on the other hand. Thus it is not at all clear that employees' contributions are really income to the employees or that employers' contributions should be imputed to employees' income.

Given this situation, it is more reasonable to consider employees' and employers' contributions as taxes and not to include them in their tax base and then to treat all benefits from the social security system as income and include them in the tax base of the beneficiaries. This is the recommendation of *Blueprints*, with which many economists would be inclined to agree. A first step in implementing this recommendation was made in 1984 when one-half of the benefits were made taxable if the combined income of the taxpayer is greater than a base amount.[14] People who receive social security benefits while having no or very small income from other sources probably will not be greatly affected by the taxation of benefits under the income tax system because for them benefits almost surely will be less than or at most close to the sum of personal exemptions and the standard deduction.

There are always some special reasons that can be given to justify and maintain a particular tax expenditure. But once we allow a special reason to justify one tax expenditure, it becomes extremely difficult to say why other tax expenditures should not be justified for some other special reason. Thus it is fairly clear that the most satisfactory solution to this problem is to eliminate virtually all tax expenditures, except those cases where there exist some major measurement or other problems raising serious administrative difficulties. Even in these cases, every effort should be made to recapture the income so excluded from the tax base, perhaps at a later date, as described for unrealized capital gains.

Bradley-Gephardt Proposal for Tax Reform (Individual Income Tax)

Outline of the Proposal

The first truly comprehensive analysis of the current federal individual and corporate income taxes and their reform was contained in *Blueprints for Basic Tax Reform*, prepared in 1977.[15] This document was meant to be a comprehensive survey of analytical issues, and it contains invaluable information on many of the issues of tax reform.

During the past two years, members of Congress have introduced a number of specific proposals for tax reform.[16] Of these proposals, one by Senator Bradley and Congressman Gephardt and another by Congressman Kemp and Senator Kasten seem to be the two major contenders as of now.

The K-K proposal would eliminate a number of tax expenditures but retain some popular deductions and exclusions, leaving the broadening of the tax base incomplete. It would increase personal exemptions to $2,000 per capita and eliminate extra exemptions for the elderly and the blind. It would allow a standard deduction of $2,600 for single taxpayers and $3,500 for married taxpayers. Beyond that, all income would be taxed at a flat 25 percent rate; however, 20 percent of salary income under the social security wage base ($37,800 per worker in 1984) would be excluded from the tax base. Therefore the effective marginal rate for this portion of income would be 20 percent. Above the social security wage base the excluded income would be added back into income at a 12.5 percent rate; therefore the effective marginal rate for this range of income would be slightly over 28 percent. After this add-back is completed, the effective rate would decrease to the standard 25 percent. All investment income would be taxed at a constant 25 percent.

Sponsors of the K-K proposal state that adoption of their proposal would leave the federal revenue essentially unaffected. We are not in a position to confirm this claim from our own rough calculations based on what we know of this proposal. They also state that this proposal will leave the distributional burden of the federal individual income taxes essentially unchanged from the current system. Although it is true that substantial progressivity is maintained under this proposal at the low end of the income distribution because of the sizable increase in personal exemptions and standard deductions, upper-income groups (those whose income is above the point at which the effective rate reverts to 25 percent) seem to be favored. We cannot be sure of these conclusions, however, because to the best of our knowledge there exists no publicly available detailed analysis of the revenue and distributional impacts of the K-K proposal on which the statements by sponsors are based, thus depriving us of the natural starting point for our own analysis of the revenue and distributional implications of this proposal. For these reasons we focus attention primarily on the B-G proposal.[17]

The B-G proposal revises both the individual and corporate income tax systems. This chapter is concerned with only the individual income tax system. In the current political discussion, the issue of reforming the tax system to make it more acceptable in terms of equity, efficiency, and simplicity is closely intertwined with the problem of raising more revenues for the federal government so as to reduce the very large deficits in the federal budget. These two issues are, however, conceptually separable, and the B-G proposal explicitly addresses only the question of tax reform, not the problems of raising additional revenues.

The B-G proposal for revising the individual income tax

system contains four parts. The first part is to eliminate or to reduce substantially a large number of special provisions that reduce the tax base, the so-called tax expenditures. The table in appendix A presents the detailed dispositions proposed by the B-G package of expenditure items listed in the Joint Committee on Taxation–Congressional Budget Office analysis. The B-G proposal, if adopted, will eliminate roughly one-half of the dollar amount of the tax expenditures in the individual income tax system as identified by the joint committee. Thus roughly $110 billion of revenue will be recovered.

Second, personal exemptions will be increased to $1,600 for the taxpayer and spouse but remain at the level of $1,000 for all other dependents. The standard deduction (or the zero bracket amount) will also increase from $2,300 to $3,000 for single returns and from $3,400 to $6,000 for joint returns.

Third, the tax rate schedule will be greatly simplified, and the regular tax rate will be 14 percent throughout the entire income ranges. In addition, surtaxes will be imposed for higher-income brackets, as follows:

Adjusted gross income	Surtax rate single returns	Combined tax rate
Below $25,000	No surtax	14%
$25,000–37,500	12%	26%
Over $37,500	16%	30%

Adjusted gross income	Surtax rate joint returns	Combined tax rate
Below $40,000	No surtax	14%
$40,000–65,000	12%	26%
Over $65,000	16%	30%

(For married persons filing separately, the tax brackets would be half of the joint return tax brackets.)

Fourth, the proposal will compute the regular tax (at 14 percent) on the basis of adjusted gross income (AGI) less deductions and exemptions. Surtaxes will be computed on the basis of adjusted gross income without applying any deductions or exemptions.

It is also stated that the indexing of the tax system to adjust for the general price inflation, currently scheduled to become effective in 1985, will be repealed.

Base-Broadening Measures

Many of the tax expenditure items may appear to be justified at some time and for some specific groups, but they are not easy to justify when considered in their entirety. Thus the elimination of the exclusions and deductions proposed by the B-G bill appears to be well justified.

An important question is whether Bradley and Gephardt have gone far enough. This is especially important for the excluded items because they will be excluded from the base of both the regular tax and the surtax, while deducted items, in the B-G proposal, will be excluded from the base of the regular tax but not from the base of the surtax. From the purely economic point of view, it is desirable to eliminate virtually all tax expenditures and tax all income from all sources as equally as possible.

From the practical point of view, however, there are some cases where such an objective is extremely difficult to achieve. For instance, it is difficult to tax the employer contribution to pension funds because, especially in the case of defined benefit plans, it is difficult to measure the consequent accretion to the net worth of the employees. Although it is desirable to tax capital gains on an accrual basis, frequently it is difficult to obtain a precise measure of the tax base unless the asset is sold. In some cases, such as interest payments on mortgages, the political pressure for retaining this preferred tax treatment may be too great. Given these conditions the B-G proposal seems to go a reasonable distance toward reducing the amount of tax expenditures. There are, however, a few obvious and significant omissions.

First, the retention of the exclusion provision for capital gains at death is open to serious question, especially if the capital gains are to be taxed at ordinary rates otherwise. This would induce many relatively wealthy individuals to arrange their assets in such a way that those assets on which they have accumulated large capital gains would be left to their beneficiaries. This may become less serious if the current law on gifts and estate tax is strengthened. In addition, the primary justification for retaining the exclusion provision for interest payments on new state and local general obligation bonds is political; however, political pressures might be neutralized substantially by offering state and local government some increases in revenue-sharing funds.[18]

There is no justification for allowing the deductibility of charitable contributions at the so-called current market value, particularly if it is inflated. A plausible rule that would eliminate this loophole would be to require that the deduction of a charitable contribution of a marketable item be either at its acquisition cost, properly depreciated, or at the realizable market value, whichever is less, and that the deduction for a charitable contribution of a nonmarketable item be at its acquisition cost, again properly depreciated.[19]

The largest item that could easily be included but remains mostly excluded is represented by social security benefits. A beginning has been made toward the inclusion of benefits. Any broadening of the benefits to be included in the income tax base would improve the tax system from the viewpoints of economic efficiency and equity. There may be, however, good reason to make the employee contribution to social insurance deductible, perhaps gradually over time as benefits are brought into the tax base.

Exemptions and Standard Deductions

The personal exemption has been declining since the 1950s in real terms and especially relative to per capita income. This decline has contributed as much as has the gradual moderation in the schedule of the marginal tax rates to the loss of progressivity in the income tax system over these years. Thus it seems proper to increase the level of personal exemptions at this time. But the B-G proposal does considerably more than that. Because all surtaxes are computed on the basis of the adjusted gross income before deduction or exemptions, exemptions become not the deductions in the usual sense but effectively a credit against the tax, in the amount of $224 ($1,600 $\times$ 0.14) for the taxpayer and spouse and of $140 for remaining dependents. Thus the tax advantage of, say, $1,000 of exemption remains the same before and after the adoption of the proposal for a relatively low-income taxpayer whose applicable marginal rate is 14 percent, but for those taxpayers in higher-income brackets who face much higher marginal tax rates, the exemption would be worth much less after the adoption of the reform than it was before its adoption. A similar observation applies to the standard deduction.

This change in treatment of personal exemption and standard deductions, along with the increase in their size, should contribute somewhat toward increasing the progressivity of the tax system. This is a counterpart to the reduction of the progressivity caused by the lowering of the marginal rates of the tax for higher-income taxpayers, which is inevitable whenever an attempt is made to flatten the tax rate over all income ranges.

Since both personal exemptions and standard deductions are given effectively as credits against the gross tax liability under the B-G proposal, it seems preferable to make them explicitly credits rather than deductions applicable only for computing the regular tax. By doing so, the distinction between the regular tax and surtaxes becomes unnecessary for filers who do not itemize, and computations of the net tax liability can be simplified.

The Rate Structure

The rate structure of the B-G proposal seems to be an attempt to compromise between the desire to have a flat, relatively low tax rate, and not to make the tax system regressive. To the extent that the top marginal rate is lowered to 30 percent from the present 50 percent, the gross effect of the change in the marginal rate must be to make the tax system more regressive than without the change. There are, however, two counteracting changes. First, the elimination of roughly half of tax expenditure items (in terms of the dollar amount) tends to make the tax system more progressive because these tax expenditure items by and large benefit middle- to higher-income taxpayers. Second, the fact that the personal exemption and standard deduction are increased and that they are deductible only for the purpose of computing the regular tax but not in computing the surtax also contributes to the progressivity of the system.

The B-G proposal as a whole, according to its sponsors, will leave both the total revenue from the individual income tax system and its distributional effects among broad income groups roughly unchanged in 1983 from those generated by the currently effective tax laws.[20] Based on our computations, these claims by the sponsors of the proposal seem, with some qualification, to be valid within a reasonable range of approximation.

A basic question that must be raised about the tax rate structure in the B-G proposal is whether it is desirable to have just three brackets. Once we are prepared to have different rates for different brackets, no matter how few the number of brackets, taxpayers will still have to compute their taxes using a tax table. On the other hand, to be meaningful, the rate schedule such as that in the B-G proposal must have at least one significant jump. In their case, at $25,000 for single persons and $40,000 for married couples filing joint returns, the rate jumps from 14 percent to 26 percent. Such a jump potentially can have a significant disrupting effect on some taxpayers' decisions. It seems, therefore, that there is little to be lost by having a gradual increase in tax rates; for example, the second bracket may be divided into four brackets of equal width, and the rate may be raised 3 percent at a time rather than by 12 percent in a single jump. While avoiding the disruption associated with a large jump in rates, such a graduated pattern will not have any additional disincentive effects or cause any additional inefficiencies. Furthermore such a smooth, gradual increase in tax rates should provide an additional small element of progressivity.

Indexing for General Price Inflation

The B-G proposal eliminates the indexing scheduled to become effective in 1985 under the current tax law. When the inflation rate is high, a tax system defined in nominal terms creates many serious distortions in the economy. The bracket creeping effect, which the scheduled indexing provision under the current code addresses, is only one of these distortions. The misrepresentation of depreciation charges is another well-known problem. Finally, flows of nominal interest become inappropriate as a basis of taxation because part of the interest represents a payment for loss of purchasing power of the principal. Capital gains and losses on assets and liabilities should also be net of general price level changes if they are properly to be included in the tax base.[21]

To the extent possible, it is desirable to define the U.S. tax code in real terms by introducing a careful, systematic indexing system. A detailed design of such an indexing system is beyond the scope of this book, but one significant and often neglected consideration should be mentioned: it is important that any indexing that may be undertaken in the economy be based on a correct price index. This index should be a variable-weighted, value-added price index, net of indirect business taxes, and not the final goods price index such as the consumer price index (CPI). A choice of an incorrect price index as the base has caused serious difficulties in other countries where indexing has been tried, such as Belgium, Italy, and Israel.[22]

Overall Revenue and Distributional Impacts

In order to understand the basis of the assertions made by sponsors of the B-G proposal that the proposed changes leave the total revenue and distributional impacts of the current federal individual income tax code roughly unchanged, we have carried out some detailed calculations based on the available data and using the set of assumptions commonly used by the government and congressional experts in making these types of analyses. The details are reported in appendixes A and B.

Insofar as the total revenue impact is concerned, our analysis confirms the statement by the sponsors of the B-G proposal that the overall impact of the proposed changes is to leave the total revenue collected under the current code roughly unchanged in 1983. In later years it is probable that the B-G proposal will increase the total revenue moderately, since under current law, tax expenditure items would increase more rapidly than the income base.

In order to estimate the distributional impacts, many stronger assumptions are necessary, and we find that such results are likely to be less certain than the overall revenue impact. Since our computations confirmed the revenue estimate claimed by the sponsors of the B-G proposal, which in turn is based on a careful analysis by congressional experts, it seems reasonable to accept the claim that this proposal leaves the distributional impact of the current tax laws unchanged as a first rough approximation. A flat structure of marginal tax rates over income groups, however, tends to place heavier burdens of tax on the middle-income groups and a lighter burden on low- and high-income groups relative to a graduated marginal tax structure. This suspicion is reinforced by the information on effective average tax rates by adjusted gross income classes implied by the rate schedule in the B-G proposal, shown in appendix table B.2. To be sure, figures in this table do not take account of effects of base-broadening measures in the proposal, but there is always the possibility that the proposal may moderately affect the current distribution of the tax burden by shifting some of the burden from the low- and high-income classes toward the middle-income class.

It should be possible to reduce this potential effect if the rate structure of the B-G proposal is altered so that the marginal tax rate rises gradually from 14 percent to 30 percent rather than in two abrupt shifts. In order to compensate for a slight loss in revenue due to such a change, it may turn out to be necessary to increase the top rate by another 1 percent or so. Such a change toward a more gradual rise in the marginal rate does not seem to present any serious undesirable feature, and it has an added advantage that it may reduce possible distortions in economic decisions due to the presence of two sizable shifts in the marginal rate, one very large.

Transitional Problems

Any major revision of tax laws will have complex and sometimes serious one-time effects on some taxpayers. When a provision giving special favored treatment to a specific type of asset is eliminated from the tax law, there will, in addition to the basic effect, almost always be a decline in the market value of the asset. Certain contractual arrangements—for instance, between employers and employees—that were economical for both parties under the older law may no longer make sense under the new law and may have to be revised at substantial costs. A person may have trained for a particular occupation because there was some significant advantage in that occupation under some provisions of the tax law, which may become unavailable due to the revision of the law, and so on.

Although it is customary in revising tax laws to take account of these problems and to minimize undue hardships and unwarranted gains, it is impossible to eliminate these problems entirely, and some windfall losses and gains, within reason, must be tolerated whenever any revision of tax laws is undertaken. Two frequently used devices can reduce these windfall gains and losses due to tax law changes. The first is to introduce the change gradually over time, either through a number of incremental changes or to set the effective date of the change considerably later than the time of enactment so that taxpayers may have time to prepare for the change. The second is the so-called grandfather clause, providing that income generated through the contracts existing at the time of the tax revision would be treated under the older tax law until the expiration of the contract in question or until some specified date, whichever comes first.

Although the B-G proposal is silent on the question of these problems, there is no question that the revision of the tax code of the magnitude contemplated by this proposal will create some major transitional problems. In some cases these problems can be treated by the devices referred to. Although the B-G proposal does not make the interest from state and local general obligation bonds taxable, if it is desired to do so, such a revision could be made to apply only to newly issued bonds, leaving the existing bonds tax exempt until they mature. The treatment of employer-provided health insurance premiums as taxable income could be made effective three or four years hence, so that there would be sufficient time for employment contracts to be adjusted. Since the B-G proposal makes capital gains fully taxable at realization, those who acquire windfall capital gains as the result of other features of the bill would be taxed whether or not these gains are realized, provided that capital gains are fully taxed at death.

One fairly major problem is associated with the treatment of both interest payments on mortgages and real estate taxes. Under the B-G proposal, the former will be deductible only for regular taxes at 14 percent, while the latter will no longer be deductible. Not only will home owners find that the cost of owning a house has increased, but they may also find that market values of their homes have declined.[23] Taking care of these and other transitional problems solely through timing of effective dates or through grandfather clauses would be quite difficult for two reasons: the problem would be pervasive throughout the economy; and the revision of the tax rate schedule would have to be timed carefully so that significant total losses to the individuals involved or to the government will not take place.

Given these considerations, a fairly attractive alternative is to use the minimum tax provision of the existing tax law as the transition device. The minimum tax provision of the existing law was substantially strengthened in 1982 to include more previously excluded items in the base of the minumum tax, so that a reasonably solid basis on which to build already exists under the current tax code. It is still necessary to add to this base a number of additional items, as Graetz points out.[24] But the strengthening of the minimum tax provision, perhaps over several years, should not cause as many transitional problems as a complete and immediate shift to the tax system envisioned in the B-G proposal. Once the base of the minimum tax is made approximately the same as the one defined in the B-G proposal, raising the tax rate from the current 20 percent to a somewhat higher level should not present any severe transitional problems, and from there it would be relatively easy to move to the final tax system.

One useful indirect benefit of using the minimum tax provision as the transition device is that, while this provision is made increasingly effective, the tax authority will be able to collect critically important information for estimating the effects of the tax reform. For instance, at the present time, the dollar amounts of income currently excluded from the income tax base, both in total and by income classes, must be inferred from information obtained from indirect and sometimes unreliable sources. Thus estimates of impacts of the B-G proposal are subject to a sizable margin of error. Information collected through the administration of the strengthened minimum tax provision would reduce this uncertainty substantially.

Social Security System

Any major tax reform should consider the relationship between the federal individual income tax system and the
social security program. In 1983 the estimated total revenue from federal individual income taxes was $295.8 bil-
lion, and total receipts from the social security taxes
amounted to $234.4 billion (national income and product
account basis). Roughly half of the revenue from the social
security system consists of employer contributions; even
excluding this portion, however, social security taxes constitute close to a third of the total revenue from the personal income tax system, and therefore any analysis of
individual income taxes excluding the social security tax is
incomplete.

If the social security system (we are here specifically re-
ferring to the old age and survivor's insurance program) is
strictly an insurance program, it would be appropriate to
include the contributions to it in the tax base of individuals
on whose behalf the contribution is made and to exclude
the benefits paid by the system from the income tax base.
But the system is far from an insurance program. It is much
more accurate to describe it as a tax and transfer system, in
which contributions by individuals and their employers
have only the vaguest of relationships to the benefits they
eventually receive. On the contribution side it is clear that
the system is regressive. On the benefit side the system is
progressive and is especially helpful to taxpayers who
have earned modest income during most of their working
lives and lack other sources of income after their retirement. For older taxpayers who have substantial income
from other sources, the system contributes additional income at a reduced tax rate and hence has some regressive
tendency.

The most logical way to improve the horizontal and vertical equity characteristics of the combined individual income tax and social security system from the purely economic point of view is to incorporate the social security tax completely into the individual income tax system and treat the benefits as income and include them in the tax base. It is probably the case, however, that such a radical change in the system is not politically feasible.

Under the circumstances the following alternative is offered as an example of an approach that would substantially improve the current system and could be retained more or less intact under the B-G proposal. First, all income, both from labor and from capital, roughly defined as adjusted gross income in the B-G proposal, rather than the first $40,000 of wages, would be made subject to social security tax. The contribution rate would then be lowered to keep the total revenue of the system approximately unchanged. Second, social security tax payments would then be made deductible from the tax base, as are other deductible items in the B-G proposal. Third, benefits from the old age and survivor's insurance program would be included in the base of the individual income tax system. Such a reform should improve the horizontal and vertical equity of the individual income tax–social security system and also improve the financial stability of the social security fund.[25]

The Medicare portion of this system, however, is much closer to a health insurance system and should be treated accordingly. As a result, economic and equity considerations would support the inclusion of not only the employee contribution but also the employer contribution in the tax base of the individual on whose behalf the contribution is made.

Summary

Insofar as we have been able to replicate the analysis on which the B-G proposal is based, the adoption of this proposal, preferably with some changes, should improve the federal individual income tax system relative to the current law from the point of view of horizontal and vertical equity, efficiency, simplicity, and most other standard criteria commonly used in judging a tax system.[26]

To realize the goals of the B-G proposal, it is important that the base-broadening measures currently incorporated into the proposal be adopted as a whole. If some of these measures are omitted from the proposal, the resulting tax system may change the tax incidence as planned under the proposal and might introduce or perpetuate economic inefficiencies.

If it becomes politically impossible to adopt the B-G proposal in its entirety and substantial dilution of that proposal takes place, an entirely different alternative should be considered. A further strengthening of the minimum tax provision could be used as an attractive transition device toward the adoption of a system like the B-G proposal. Such a step could also be considered as an end in itself, since it would improve the equity of the current tax code and contribute to increasing the federal revenue somewhat. The base of the minimum tax could then be made more and more complete, and it could also be made applicable to ever lower income classes. This would increase the total revenue from the tax system, allowing the reduction of marginal rates and some increases in personal exemptions. It should be possible to approach a system fairly similar to the one envisioned in the B-G proposal in this way gradually over time. Such an approach would help to minimize the risk of unintended distributional and economic consequences of any major change in the tax law. It may also have the effect of reducing the political resistance to a comprehensive income tax system.

5

Changes in Income-Based Taxes: Corporate Income Taxes

Rationale and Problems of Corporate Taxation

When corporations pay taxes, they do not bear the burden of the taxation. Rather the burden is borne by individuals although its precise incidence—on consumers in the form of higher prices, on labor in the form of lower wages, and on corporate stockholders and other investors in the form of lower returns on capital—is not known.[1] The net income earned by a corporation ultimately is paid to its stockholders in the form of dividends or capital gains. Thus a tax on net income of corporations does not have the same rationale as a tax on the net income of individuals. The major justification usually given for a separate corporate tax arises from the fact that the corporation is considered by law an independent entity and its owners granted limited liability. Thus it can be used by stockholders for the accumulation of undistributed and untaxed wealth and by a small number of corporate insiders for the amassing of economic power unless they are constrained by separate taxation and other legal restrictions.[2] A second common justification for the corporate tax is that it is a relatively convenient mechanism for collecting a large amount of government revenue, which alternatively would have to be collected directly from a much larger number of stockholders or other taxpayers.

The major criticism of a separate system of corporate taxation has been that since capital income generated by corporations is subject to double taxation—taxation at both the corporate and individual levels—an undue burden is placed on corporate investment.[3] Also this double taxation of corporate profits would be expected to result in a misallocation of resources with a consequent loss in economic efficiency since the taxation of business income is made to depend on the extent to which economic activities are carried out in corporate form.

Another important criticism is that under the present system of separate corporate taxation, the effective tax rates on income earned within the corporation are not related to the circumstances of the individual beneficial owners of the stock, contributing to inequities in the burden of taxation. Other objections are that the present form of corporate taxation encourages retention of corporate earnings to avoid double taxation and financing by debt rather than external equity. Debt financing takes advantage of the favorable corporate tax treatment of interest paid on debt as contrasted with dividends paid on stock. As a result, at least to some extent, the cost of capital and therefore investment decisions may depend on the form of financing used, with an adverse effect on economic efficiency.

Many of these objections to the present system of corporate taxes could be met by some form of integration of the corporate and individual income taxes, either in making the corporate tax a withholding mechanism for the individual income tax or, at the extreme, in completely abolishing corporate income taxation. There are, however, other important criticisms of the present system of corporate taxation, which at least in part are independent of the question of such integration. They relate in particular to three additional deficiencies in the current structure of corporate taxes.[4] First, greatly disparate tax rates on different investments—especially as between plant and equipment—result in allocational inefficiencies. Second, discrepancies between the taxable and economic income of corporations can be substantial in periods of high inflation, resulting during the 1970s in a level of taxable income markedly higher than economic income and in a corresponding overpayment of taxes. Third, the tax loss provisions reflect the asymmetric treatment of gains and losses under current corporate tax law, with gains immediately taxable but losses conferring no tax benefits unless or until they can be offset against gains. As a result corporations with higher recent taxable profits, which are also more likely to be taxable in the near future, generally face lower effective tax rates than other firms and thus are faced with different investment incentives.

All three of these problems could be corrected by the elimination of corporate taxes, but there may be very real costs involved in the absence of full integration of corporate and personal income taxes in which stockholders pay the equivalent of the corporate tax rate on retained earnings as well as dividends. There would be a large annual loss of revenue from the corporate sector, which might be difficult to replace without a substantial loss of progressivity in the overall tax structure.[5] A major one-time transfer of wealth would result from the cancellation of taxes deferred in prior years and subsequent taxes on profits to be derived from existing investment.[6]

Some of the problems associated with the level of corporate income taxes—notably those relating to double taxation—have become substantially less pressing in view of the historical decline in the importance of such taxes, especially during the Reagan administration.[7] This decline has been particularly marked for marginal rates on most new investments (table 2.13).[8] Less progress has been made on the elimination of distortions in capital allocations caused by the very large variation in effective corporate tax rates for different corporate activities and investments (tables 2.13 to 2.15). But even here there was a marked decrease in 1982 in the estimated within- and between-industry distortions due to differences in corporate tax rates.[9]

It is still true, however, that with accelerated depreciation and the investment tax credit frequently approximating immediate write-off of a new asset, the deduction of borrowing costs at the marginal corporate tax rate of 46 percent may result in a negative effective tax rate on new investment. This essentially provides a subsidy to business to undertake capital expenditures without economic justification.

Similarly the problems caused by discrepancies between the taxable and economic income of corporations have been reduced, though by no means eliminated, by both more liberal depreciation policies and a substantial abatement of inflationary pressures. Limited progress has been made on rationalizing tax loss provisions, with loss carryforwards now possible for fifteen years instead of the pre-1981 seven years, to ensure to the extent possible an identity between income on which taxes are paid and the income earned over a period extending well beyond a single tax year. This more favorable treatment of tax losses, however, is still a far cry from the symmetric tax treatment of gains and losses that theoretically requires unlimited carry-forward at the cost of capital.[10]

Virtually all of these problems could be corrected by the elimination of corporate taxes but only at substantial cost in the absence of full integration of corporate and personal income taxes. Thus corporate income tax payments in spite of their diminishing relative importance still amounted to over $60 billion in 1983 (exclusive of tax payments by Federal Reserve banks).[11] Such revenues if forgone in a period of large and increasing government deficits would have to be made up in some other form. The present value of deferred taxes and subsequent taxes on future profits from existing investment that would have been owed to the government by corporations on the basis of their existing investment was estimated to have amounted to $427 billion in 1981, which, if cancelled, would provide an extremely large windfall profit to stockholders even after allowance for future capital gains taxes.[12]

This estimate of the present value of accrued corporate taxes predicates, however, that stockholders (and the general market) assume the continuation of the current statutory rate of corporate taxes on existing assets so that a substantial reduction in this rate would be associated with substantial capital gains.[13] Whether stockholders assume the continuation of the current statutory rate of corporate taxes on existing assets in their capitalization of the expected future flow of after-tax corporate earnings on existing or new investment is open to question. On the other hand the rational pricing of stocks does require the projection of expected tax rates, and current rates are an obvious basis for such a projection.[14]

Even if stockholders do realize a large windfall profit from elimination of or substantial reduction in corporate taxes, there is still the issue of what the government should do about such windfall profit. Thus a decline in personal tax rates would be expected to be reflected in capital losses on tax-exempt bonds and other personal tax shelters, but historically owners of such assets have not been compensated or penalized for capital losses or gains associated with changes in these rates. Similarly, stockholders historically have not been reimbursed or assessed for the adverse or favorable effects on stock values of changes in statutory corporate tax rates. The appropriate treatment of unexpected capital gains and losses associated with changes in tax legislation depends on whether the gain or loss is regarded as the favorable or unfavorable outcome of normal business risk or as an abnormal event with such serious consequences for the firms affected or other sectors of the economy as to require special government measures to mitigate these consequences.

Specific Proposals for Reform

Bradley-Gephardt

The first proposal for reform of the current system of corporate income taxes that we shall consider is that contained in the Bradley-Gephardt proposal. The major provisions of the proposal as it applies to corporations are the imposition of a uniform tax rate of 30 percent for all corporations, the repeal of most existing tax deductions, credits, and exemptions that distort investment decisions, and a new depreciation system that does not discriminate among types of assets but attempts to ensure the equivalence of book and economic depreciation.[15] The total amount of revenues that would have been raised in 1983 by the proposed system of corporate taxes is estimated to be about the same as that raised by the current system. The decrease in corporate revenues attributable to the reduction in the basic statutory corporate tax rates from the present 46 percent for all but the very small corporations to the proposed 30 percent for all corporations would be approximately offset by the $43.8 billion estimated increase in revenues (see appendix A) resulting from the elimination of investment tax credits, accelerated depreciation allowances, and a large number of other existing tax deductions.[16] Thus Bradley-Gephardt is not designed to change significantly either the magnitude of the federal deficit or the progressivity of the tax structure.

The major improvement in corporate taxation would be the elimination of the unequal tax treatment of different corporations and investment activities, a step that should result in improved equity and allocational efficiency. The elimination of tax incentives that encourage the use of certain types of capital over others and of capital over noncapital productive inputs would be expected to increase economic efficiency. The changes in depreciation policy under B-G would not only improve allocational efficiency by eradicating the distortions mandated by current tax law but would also simplify depreciation reporting by corporate taxpayers; depreciation under the proposed legislation would be computed by broad asset life classes rather than separately for each asset.

Some economists would take exception and argue that the elimination of much of the current preferential tax treatment of new corporate investment is an undesirable feature of the B-G proposal. This argument stems from a perceived need to increase new investment, productivity, and economic growth. Currently, marginal tax rates for corporations are on average much lower than average tax rates, which would be expected to stimulate investment at least in the short run. While such stimulation of capital formation by special tax incentives to new investment may well be effective for the short run and desirable in a period of recession and underutilization of resources, there is less justification for it in the longer run. For corporate investment to increase in the short run or long run, either total saving or the share of corporate investment in total private investment would have to increase. There is no reason why special tax incentives to new corporate investment should affect total saving significantly so that such incentives would have to operate largely through their depressant effect on private noncorporate investment, mainly housing.[17]

In the long run under present (or any similar) law, the

differences between the marginal and average tax rates would greatly diminish, and the cost of capital on new investments might be substantially increased as corporations factored in the uncertainty of changes in the capital value of the firm's existing assets associated with uncertain changes in further tax incentives on new investments. Thus it is interesting to note that when corporate officials are asked for the most effective tax changes for purposes of stimulating plant and equipment outlays with the same reduction in government revenues, they indicate that a general decrease in the rate of corporate taxes, such as that provided in the B-G proposal, would be nearly as effective as a permanent increase in the investment tax credit or liberalization of depreciation.[18]

The other deficiencies in the current system of corporate taxes seem to be attenuated by the B-G changes. The new legislation like the present law does not relate the effective tax rates on incomes earned within the corporation to the circumstances of the individual stockholder. This becomes much less important, however, given the changes in the effective tax rates for both individuals and corporations, which greatly narrow the range of personal tax rates and create a uniform maximum tax rate for both individuals and corporations. Discrepancies between the taxable and economic incomes of corporations would also generally be reduced though they might still be substantial in periods of extreme inflation or deflation. The inadequacies of the current corporate tax loss provisions would still remain in Bradley-Gephardt but in somewhat diluted form. This improvement would reflect the lower statutory tax rates for most corporate investment, the closer coincidence of tax and economic depreciation, and the reduction in the importance of accelerated depreciation in the early years prior to the existence of adequate profits against which any losses can be charged.[19]

As for the effect of Bradley-Gephardt on corporate financial policy, the personal tax provisions in the proposed law would discourage the current practice of retaining corporate earnings to minimize taxes because of a substantial reduction in the differential between the personal tax rates on ordinary income and capital gains. It might also diminish somewhat the incentives for corporations to engage in debt financing because of the smaller tax advantage associated with the lower nominal tax rate on corporate income. However, this effect of the lower corporate tax rate on the relative costs of debt and equity capital could be offset at least in part by the greater reduction in personal tax rates applicable to interest income than in those applicable to the total return (dividends and capital gains combined) on equity investment.[20] In addition the enactment of Bradley-Gephardt might be associated with changes in the level and structure of interest rates, which may have other significant effects on corporate retention and debt-equity policy.

The proposed changes in the corporate tax laws may result in sizable transitional costs and benefits for many corporations. At least initially some corporations would be paying significantly more taxes (others significantly less) than they would under current law, but the amounts paid would correspond much more closely to those appropriate under an equitable and economically efficient assessment of taxes. The companies paying more taxes generally would be those that previously benefited most from preferential tax treatment. Moreover, since Bradley-Gephardt grandfathers tax expenditure items applicable to capital outlays prior to the enactment of the proposed legislation, the one-time capital losses involved for individual corporations should generally not be large.

The essentially equity argument for such grandfathering is stated in *Blueprints*:

In general, the repeal of code provisions that provide an incentive for certain business-related expenditures or investments in specific assets should be developed to minimize the losses to persons who make such expenditures or investments prior to the effective date of the new law. The principal technique to effectuate this policy would be to grandfather actions taken under current law. For example, any repeal of a tax credit (such as the investment tax credit) and any requirement that an expenditure that is currently deductible (such as soil and water conservation expenditures) must be capitalized should be prospective only. . . . Unused tax credits earned in pre-effective date years should be available as a carryover to taxable years after the effective date to the extent allowed under current law. The repeal of special provisions allowing accelerated amortization or depreciation of certain assets generally should apply only with respect to expenditures made or assets placed in service after a specific cutoff date. The revised general depreciation and depletion rules should apply to property placed in service or expenditures made after an effective date.[21]

Yet arguments can be raised against such grandfathering. It is not clear that corporations and the stock market do, or have the right to, capitalize the current structure of taxes in estimating the present value of their future tax liabilities. Investment tax credits on new investment, depreciation policy, and statutory tax rates have all been subject to changes historically.[22] Grandfathering has generally (but not universally) been applied to investment tax credits and depreciation policy on capital outlays made prior to enactment of the new law but not to those made subsequently; grandfathering has not been applied to statutory tax ratios. The B-G proposed legislation implicitly assumes that corporate and market expectations have legitimately been based on the continued preferential treatment of the pre-B-G tax expenditure items on capital outlays made prior to enactment of the new law. It further assumes that an equivalent assumption is not warranted to justify continued application of such preferential treatment on subsequent capital outlays.

Estimates made by the technical staff of the Joint Committee on Taxation and the Congressional Budget Office suggest that the B-G elimination of tax preferences on new investment and the associated reduction in the statutory corporate tax rates approximately offset each other both currently and for the next few years. The reduction in the statutory corporate tax rates by about one-third would persist after the tax preference on old investments had been charged off. Although the present value of the subsequent tax losses would be greatly dampened by the currently high level of interest rates, the enactment of Bradley-Gephardt would still entail at least a moderate cancellation in the implicit debt owed the government, resulting in a significant capital gain by corporations as a whole. This assumes, as would appear to be reasonable, that there is little justification for believing that corporations and the market had been projecting the continued availability of tax preference items on investments not yet made.

It is clear that most corporations would benefit significantly and others would be significantly hurt in the transitional process, unless remedial provisions are enacted. Changes in the special corporate or personal tax treatment currently affecting certain industries in particular, such as real estate and mineral resources, would be expected to cause significant losses in the capital values of companies in these industries. Capital losses associated with the reduction or elimination of preferential tax treatment would be larger for long-term than for short-term assets and largest for assets specific to a given corporation or industry or for assets whose supply can be altered only slowly.[23] What is not clear is the optimal transitional policy to handle these problem cases.

If an attempt is made to safeguard companies completely

from capital losses associated with the new legislation, it would be desirable to recoup for the government the capital gains achieved by other companies, not only on equity grounds but also to guard against further erosion in government revenues. It might be possible, though extremely difficult, to set up rules for achieving this objective through a system of transitional credits and surtaxes; however, a much easier approach to the problems resulting from the B-G changes in corporate taxation would be a phasing-in period of perhaps five years, for which corporations initially could select either the old or new legislation as the basis for taxation. The latter approach, though simpler to implement, would not serve as an absolute safeguard for every company against any capital losses resulting from the change in corporate tax law and would be associated with considerable loss in tax revenues over the transitional period.

A third approach is to view the effects of changes in tax laws not otherwise provided for in B-G as a normal business risk and to make no or very limited provisions for these additional transitional problems. The approach followed will be partly determined by tax philosophy and views on what future tax expectations are capitalized in stock prices but also by the relative weights placed on equity, simplicity, and concern about the government deficit. Therefore it would be useful to have more information than seems to be currently available about the quantitative impact of the proposed tax changes on different types of companies as well as on corporations as a whole.

Finally, the adoption of the B-G proposals would not only improve the functioning of the corporate tax system at this time but would facilitate the possibility of integration of corporate and personal taxes in the future since the elimination of tax preferences available to corporations would help ensure a closer relationship between economic or true income of corporations and their reported income.

Although the B-G proposed changes in corporate taxation are an improvement over current law, they still leave considerable room for further improvement in several respects. First, the double taxation remaining in B-G still taxes disproportionately the stock-related form of capital income (though the favorable treatment of unrealized capital gains represents a partial offset). Second, the corporate taxes on such income are not levied equitably among stockholders in different income groups. Third, the approximate coincidence of book and economic depreciation that the proposed legislation attempts to achieve is predicated on a 6 percent annual inflation rate, and major disparities between the two depreciation figures would appear if inflation flared up again or disappeared. Moreover no adjustment is made for the effect of inflation on the real burden of the corporate debt. Fourth, inadequate provisions for tax loss still persist. Of these deficiencies the first two can be corrected by integration of corporate and personal income taxes. The last two can be greatly alleviated by measures designed to ensure a closer coincidence of economic and book income over time. These measures include explicitly tying in allowed depreciation for tax purposes to the rate of inflation;[24] adjusting corporate income for inflation-induced changes both in the real interest paid on and in the real value of long-term corporate debt; and permitting unlimited carry-forwards of losses against future profits.[25]

Of the two inflation adjustments, that for depreciation is the more basic in view of the magnitudes involved. The absence of such an adjustment was an important factor in explaining the adverse effect of unexpected inflation on corporate economic profits and stock prices in the inflationary period of the 1970s.[26] On the other hand unexpected inflation also significantly reduces the burden of corporate debt, especially long-term debt, so that an adjustment for depreciation alone overstates the effect of unexpected inflation on economic income. Economic and equity considerations support both types of inflation adjustment. Still, if the debt adjustment is unduly cumbersome, an adjustment for depreciation alone would appear to be preferable to no adjustment at all.

Even with the problems associated with the proposed B-G legislation and possible changes in the present version of that proposal, in our judgment Bradley-Gephardt, with or without these changes, represents an improvement over current tax law.[27]

Integration of Corporate and Personal Income Taxes

A satisfactory integration of corporate and personal income taxes would eliminate most of the problems associated with the present system of corporate taxation or with the revised system under Bradley-Gephardt. Such integration can be accomplished in a number of ways.[28] A theoretically satisfactory approach—and one consistent with considerations of equity and allocational efficiency—would be to abolish corporate taxation and to allocate corporate income on a pro rata basis to the stockholders. Such an allocation would essentially treat corporations as though they were partnerships. A basic problem with this approach is that stockholders would be taxed on corporate income that had not been distributed to them, frequently raising serious liquidity difficulties and requiring substantial liquidation of stock, a significant part of it relatively unmarketable. Another problem relates to the appropriate taxation of income on shares owned by foreigners and tax-free institutions. An obvious way of avoiding these problems would be to have the corporations pay the taxes on their income at the corporate tax rate, which under Bradley-Gephardt would be set at the maximum personal tax rate paid by stockholders. As a result the potential liquidity difficulties would disappear, but stockholders as a whole in the absence of credits against personal taxes would be indirectly paying a higher corporate tax rate than warranted by their weighted average personal tax rate, with the excess largest for the lower-income groups and institutions.

An approach that would avoid both the equity and liquidity problems would be to have the corporations notify the individual taxpayers about their pro rata share of corporate income and of the taxes paid on their behalf by the corporation. Individual taxpayers would be taxed on their share of corporate income and given tax credits for their share of taxes paid. This would result in an excess of tax credits over their pro rata share of corporate income for the low-income shareholders and institutions, and under Bradley-Gephardt an equivalence of tax credits and pro rata share of corporate income for the upper-income shareowners. Without some further adjustment, this approach would lower the total tax revenue collected under Bradley-Gephardt as a result of an effective rate of taxation on corporate income below the B-G corporate tax rate of 30 percent.[29] However, some tax experts are convinced that such full integration would be impractical for various reasons, including the need to allocate profits and losses among part-year and full-year shareholders and to allocate changes in return arising from audits or other adjustments for earlier tax years.[30]

Other tax experts, such as those participating in the preparation of the Treasury *Blueprints for Basic Tax Reform*, advocate the elimination of the corporate income tax (except as a withholding device) and the full integration of corporate and personal taxes. Such integration is advocated, however, only in the context of a comprehensive income tax reform based on a broadening of the tax base, including the treatment of capital gains as ordinary income and the elimination of the special treatment of other tax expenditures. A Special Committee of the American Bar Association (ABA) also favors adoption of full integration if the United States were to adopt "a comprehensive income tax base, low rate system, as proposed by *Blueprints*."[31]

Blueprints for Basic Tax Reform makes a number of detailed suggestions for handling the administrative problems of tax integration, which generally seem feasible to carry out. As noted in *Blueprints*, however, the incorporation of a withholding tax for liquidity reasons would complicate somewhat the taxation of part-year stockholders. Also, as noted in the ABA Special Committee report, "Full integration, which would allow corporate losses to be taken without limitation by shareholders, would present the same tax shelter problems which exist with partnerships today. These require extensive and complex limitations. The problems might be even greater if such shelters were widely employed by corporations with limited liability."[32]

Blueprints recognizes that even if the administrative problems pose no insurmountable difficulties, the full integration it proposes would create serious transitional problems. Perhaps the most difficult of these is the treatment of corporate earnings that are undistributed as of the effective date of integration. *Blueprints* notes:

Under corporate integration, distributions made by a corporation to its shareholders would be tax-free to the extent of the shareholder's basis; distributions in excess of the shareholder's basis in his stock would be taxable. However, corporate earnings and profits accumulated before the effective date but distributed afterwards should not be accorded tax-free treatment; to do so would discriminate against corporations that distributed (rather than accumulated) their earnings and profits in preintegration taxable years.[33]

Blueprints proposes that current law continue to apply to dividends distributed within the next ten years to shareholders at the time of enactment (and in special cases to subsequent stockholders) if such dividends are distributed out of earnings prior to enactment. After the ten-year period all dividends would be nontaxable and would reduce the tax basis, with any amounts received in excess of basis treated as ordinary income.

In view of the administrative and transitional complexities of full integration, some form of partial integration is frequently proposed as an alternative. Under such proposals the individual income taxpayers would be provided with a deduction or credit based on their pro rata share of taxes paid by corporations on that part of their income distributed as dividends. There are two techniques for achieving partial integration, both of which involve either the elimination or reduction of the double taxation of distributed earnings. These two techniques, described in detail in the ABA Special Committee report, are the shareholder credit method applicable at the individual shareholder level and a dividend deduction method applicable at the corporate level. In the absence of conditions justifying full integration, the ABA report recommends adoption of partial integration dividend relief through a shareholder credit technique. This recommendation is largely justified on the basis of the problems posed by corporate tax preferences and by the need to treat appropriately income of U.S. investors from foreign corporations and income of foreign investors from U.S. corporations. The corporate tax preferences would largely disappear under Bradley-Gephardt; however, the problem of the appropriate treatment of investment in and from foreign countries would still remain. As the ABA report points out, probably it would be easier to handle this problem through the stockholder credit technique used by nearly all foreign countries that utilize integration systems.

The administrative and transitional difficulties under partial integration are clearly less troublesome than under full integration. It is also sometimes argued that the stimulation of dividend payout under partial integration would be desirable in that greater reliance on external equity financing would result in an increased monitoring of investment decisions by the capital markets; but on the other hand it is argued that the decline in retention of earnings would lower private saving and ultimately investment. These considerations tend to be offsetting in their welfare implications; however, one new problem is introduced. Superimposition of partial integration on a broad-based tax on personal income such as the present version of the B-G bill would lower the total personal and corporate taxes attributable to the distributed part of corporate earnings without an equivalent offset in increased revenues elsewhere, increasing the government deficit and decreasing the progressiveness of the tax structure.[34]

Another recent proposal advanced as an alternative to partial integration (the latter involving the elimination or reduction of the double taxation on all distributed earnings) is to treat "newly contributed equity capital like debt, allowing a deduction (in the corporate tax) for dividends paid up to some specified rate on the amount of capital contributed."[35] The purpose of this proposal is to remove or greatly reduce the discrimination in existing law in favor of debt over newly issued equity without incurring as much loss in revenue and progressivity as the more traditional procedures advocated for partial integration. This proposal would not allow any deduction for dividends from earnings on capital invested prior to the proposal's effective date or any deduction for dividends attributable to income from capital accumulated by retention of earnings. As contrasted to the more customary techniques for partial integration, there would be a need in implementing this proposal to distinguish between newly contributed equity and refinancing of accumulated earnings or previously contributed capital, which might raise substantial problems. Although this recent proposal involves less cost in terms of loss of revenue and progressivity than the more traditional form of partial integration, it does raise additional problems, and the net gain may not warrant the remaining loss in revenue and progressivity.[36]

There seem to be at least two feasible approaches to the ultimate full integration of corporate and personal income taxes. The first would entail the gradual reduction of corporate taxes from the 30 percent proposed by Bradley-Gephardt until they can be set at zero, offsetting a large part of the reduction in corporate taxes by the inclusion of a pro rata share of corporate retained earnings in the stockholder's personal tax base. The tax information form transmitted by the corporation to the investor would indicate not only the dividends paid to the investor but also the earnings retained on his or her behalf. Another approach would accomplish the same objective of gradually eliminating the double taxation of corporate income but retaining corporate taxation as a convenient withholding device.[37] In achieving this objective of full integration of corporate and personal income taxes, it will be necessary to ensure that total revenues to the government are not reduced, that regressivity is not introduced into the overall tax structure, and that stock owners are not provided with major windfall gains. The achievement of this objective could be complicated by the extremely large cancellation of debt implicitly owed to government by corporations. This problem would arise from the reduction of the statutory tax rate from the Bradley-Gephardt 30 percent to zero (nearly twice the Bradley-Gephardt reduction in statutory tax rates) without any offset from a reduction in tax preferences. On the other hand, the problems would be greatly reduced by the inclusion of corporate retained earnings in the stock owners' tax base as full integration is achieved. Additional study is needed to determine what further steps are required in the transitional process. Further steps, if deemed necessary, might include such measures as temporary surtaxes on corporate income or prolonged phase-in periods.

Corporate Taxes and Shifts in Tax Base from Income to Consumption

One version of a consumption-based tax is sometimes called a cash-flow tax because the accounting system used to implement it is designed to replace the current income taxes on corporations as well as individuals (including trusts). With a comprehensive consumption-based tax as with a comprehensive and fully integrated income tax, if it is not desired to impose any special tax on corporations as such, there would be no need to tax them separately.[38] Under the comprehensive consumption-based or cash-flow tax, however, it would not be necessary to impute undistributed income to individuals because taxes would be assessed only on funds available for personal consumption.

A corporate cash-flow tax is sometimes advocated in preference to the corporate income tax whether corporate income is fully or partially integrated with individual income for tax purposes. The advocates of a corporate cash-flow tax feel that there would then be no need to set up complex depreciation rules and other accounting adjustments to avoid inflation-induced distortions; there would be no windfall capital gain associated with the cancellation of future liabilities arising from future profits from existing corporate investment; it would be more difficult for individuals to use the corporate form to avoid taxation; and it would be more difficult for foreigners to escape taxation on U.S. corporate income flowing to them.[39] It is not clear to us, without more evidence than is currently available, that a corporate cash-flow tax is preferable to a corporate income tax. As long as corporations are separate entities, even in the absence of any income taxes, presumably there would be a need by corporate officials and the market for the best possible current income estimates. These would require the best possible estimates of real depreciation and of any substantial adjustments needed to reflect the effect of inflation on the corporation's economic income, though these estimates would no longer have to conform to the requirements of the Internal Revenue Service. The problem of windfall capital gains for corporations arises only when tax rates are unexpectedly reduced and in such cases can be handled in other ways.

Nor is it clear that the problem of the corporate provision of tax-free consumption for officials and employees is likely to be substantially abated by shifting from a corporate income to cash-flow tax since the basic problem in both instances is the definition of permissible corporate expenses for tax purposes.[40] Similarly as long as corporations remain separate entities and continue to prepare meaningful financial statements, it is not clear why there should be a serious problem in the collection of U.S. taxes on corporate income allocable to foreigners. The only apparent difference between the corporation income tax and the cash-flow tax in their treatment of U.S. corporate income flowing to foreigners is that the former would cover all U.S. corporate income allocable to foreigners while the latter would cover only cash distributions.

Moreover, a cash-flow tax might enable corporate officials to postpone almost indefinitely, or at least for protracted periods of time, any payment of corporate taxes as long as corporate earnings are offset by investments. Any prolonged postponement of tax payments, if sufficiently large for corporations as a whole, would contribute to the government's deficit financing problem for the foreseeable future.

Finally, the uncertainties associated with the implementation of a major new system of corporate taxation, with new and as yet unexplored possibilities for tax avoidance, suggest that a switch to the cash-flow tax might be a risky alternative to modification of the present system of corporate income taxes. The introduction of a cash-flow system of corporate taxation would also require a special transitional treatment of existing capital and debt, which might give rise to fully as difficult transitional problems as those arising from integration of personal and corporate income taxes. The case for a cash-flow corporation tax would be stronger if the present system of personal income taxes were transformed to a consumption or expenditure base. However, the adoption of a comprehensive income-based system of taxation on personal income would strengthen the case for retaining profits as the basis for corporate taxation of corporate income both before and after full integration of personal and corporate taxes is achieved.[41]

Conclusions

If income-based taxes are retained as the main basis for federal taxation, the B-G proposal as it applies to corporations as well as households seems to be a desirable first step in achieving significant progress toward the goals of simplification, equity, and economic efficiency in the overall tax structure. However, the proposal might be improved by the adoption of some additional measures that would ensure a closer coincidence between economic income and that reported for tax purposes. Beyond a somewhat modified B-G program of tax reform, we feel that full integration of corporate and personal income taxes should be the ultimate aim of an overall system of income taxation, and we have outlined several approaches to achieve this objective.

In any major revision of the tax structure, there will be significant transitional costs, but on the basis of the sketchy data available, the overall magnitude of these costs does not appear to be prohibitive for the appropriately modified B-G proposal and perhaps not even for full integration. Additional information would be highly useful to explore more satisfactorally the distribution as well as magnitude of these transitional costs. The enactment of the B-G proposal, which may be considered as a first step toward full integration of corporate and personal income taxes, would shed substantial light on the transitional costs likely to be involved in a subsequent move to full integration.

6   Consumption-Based Taxes

On occasion legislators in the United States and other interested individuals have proposed consumption-based taxes. Many reasons have been given in support of such taxes. Some have suggested that consumption-based taxes would enhance equity,[1] economic efficiency, and the level of new investment.[2] Others have suggested that such a tax would simplify the tax structure.[3] And still others believe that a consumption tax in the form of a sales tax or VAT may provide a politically easy way for the federal government to raise substantial new revenues[4] and might even help foreign trade through harmonization of the U.S. tax system with that of the Common Market.[5] Those who object to consumption-based taxes most commonly argue that such taxes would be highly regressive, as measured by ability to pay. Other arguments opposing such types of taxes range from the possible difficulties and expenses associated with collecting the tax to violations of the rights of the individual states, which traditionally have used sales taxes as a major source of revenue.

There are two types of consumption-based taxes: those collected from the buyers and those collected from producers and retailers. In turn there are two primary variants of those taxes collected from producers and sellers: the sales tax and the VAT. There are a large number of variants of each of these types of taxes. Some of these variants do not even appear at first to be consumption-based taxes but upon closer examination are indeed such. For example, the current income tax, though supposedly taxing income and not consumption, has some significant provisions that would be the same as those under some forms of a consumption-based tax.

General Arguments

The major arguments in support of a consumption-based tax over an income tax may be categorized as follows: such a tax is more equitable over time; it is conceptually easier to implement; and as a practical matter it might be expected to have fewer distortionary effects on the allocation of capital investment. The major arguments given in opposition to such a tax are that the tax may alter the distribution of the tax burden from what it is today in a regressive way; it may lead to vast accumulations of wealth by some households, and such concentration of wealth with the accompanying economic power is undesirable; it is considerably different from the current income tax, and any major movement to a consumption-based tax would give rise to severe transitional problems, including a windfall gain to younger workers who have not yet accumulated assets (such a windfall gain would be at the expense of older workers); and since consumption fluctuates less than income, it would be less stabilizing than the current income tax.

Supporting Arguments

Equity

Blueprints points out that, unlike the current system, a consumption-based tax would be neutral with respect to the timing of consumption expenditures.[6] As an example, consider two households, each with the same initial wealth and the same pattern of future wage income. Under an income tax, the present value of the future tax payments of a household that consumed less in early life and more in later life would be greater than those of a household that did the reverse, consuming more in early life and less in later life. In contrast the present value of the tax payments under a consumption-based tax with a flat rate would not vary with a household's consumption stream.[7]

Under a consumption-based tax with a flat rate, each household would pay in present value terms the same percentage of the sum of its current wealth and the present value of future wages. In short such a tax is neutral with respect to the timing of a household's consumption over time, whereas an income tax favors current consumption over future consumption. This argument would break down under a consumption-based tax with a progressive structure.[8]

Of potential interest in evaluating a consumption-based tax is that the current federal tax system contains some significant provisions expressly designed to overcome this tendency to favor current over future consumption.[9] For example, one of the express purposes of IRAs is to encourage current savings to provide for future consumption in later years. Defined-contribution plans and employee stockownership plans can be viewed as neutralizing the bias in the income tax toward current consumption.[10] There is no clear evidence that these provisions of the tax law have in fact increased savings, but nonetheless they clearly reduce the bias in the present tax law toward current consumption.

Simplicity

A consumption-based tax can avoid one major difficulty of implementing an income-based tax: the allocation of expenses incurred in one taxation period, such as a calendar

year, to produce income in subsequent taxation periods.[11]
To cope with this problem, a complex set of regulations on
depreciation of capital equipment and amortization of prepaid expenses has evolved. Under most forms of a consumption-based tax, it is not necessary to allocate expenses
in order to calculate the tax, and thus there is no need for
these regulations. For this reason a consumption-based
tax conceptually should result in a less complicated tax
system. Although this conclusion is generally correct,
consumption-based tax systems may contain some complications not present in income-based tax systems, such
as the difficulties in administering a VAT with differential
rates, as is done in Europe.

Efficiency
A consumption-based tax should have little distortionary
effect on the specific investments to which investors allocate their funds. As the Meade commission points out, one
of the major features of most consumption-based tax systems is that the before-tax rate of return on new investment is equal to the after-tax rate.[12] In contrast, a basic
feature of an income-based tax system is that the after-tax
rate of return on new investment is generally less than the
before-tax rate. The complexity and arbitrariness of actual
tax regulations make it highly unlikely that they would
produce an economically correct definition of after-tax income. For this reason some investments on an after-tax
basis undoubtedly would appear more attractive than they
should. To the extent that an income-based tax system is
simplified, the potential distortionary effects of such a system would be reduced, and simplification is one of the
primary purposes of the income tax changes already
discussed.

The difficulty of implementing an income-based tax system with an economically correct definition of after-tax in-

come may be more fundamental in that the very concept of an economically correct after-tax income may be undefined. In a world of certainty most economists could agree in principle on an economically correct definition of after-tax income, but in a world of uncertainty there might not be such agreement. In an uncertain world taxes affect both the expected return and the risk characteristics of an investment, and the definition of after-tax income would implicitly entail some trade-off between these two properties of an investment.

Although a consumption-based tax avoids some of the practical and theoretical problems of an income-based tax, it presents some problems of its own. One of the most important problems stems from the need to classify expenditures as either consumption or nonconsumption. For example, how should educational expense be classified? In addition, both consumption-based and income-based tax schemes have the common problem of measuring imputed items, such as the rental value of owner-occupied housing.

Opposing Arguments

Regressivity

A major argument against a consumption-based tax is that it is likely to reduce the progressivity present under current law. Since a consumption tax levied directly on the consumer in principle can be made as progressive as desired, this criticism strictly applies only to taxes levied on producers and retailers. Since consumption as a percentage of income declines with increases in income, a flat VAT or a flat sales tax by itself would be regressive; however, through a system of family allowances and payments and other types of tax and benefit programs, a portion of this regressivity can be reduced.

European countries that have introduced a VAT have

employed differential tax rates, with the higher rates falling on those products judged to be luxury goods. A conference of European economists sponsored by the Brookings Institute concluded that, in Europe, the VAT with differential rates combined with other features of the tax and benefit structure did not lead to an unacceptable regressivity in the tax system.[13] Nonetheless, there was wide agreement that differential rates distorted relative prices and caused administrative difficulties; therefore, it would have been preferable to have had a flat rate and to rely on other means for obtaining the desired progressivity.

Wealth Accumulation

It is clearly easier to accumulate vast wealth with the attendant economic power under a consumption-based tax than under an income-based tax. No one knows whether such accumulation would in fact occur under a consumption tax. Yet since there is at least a strong possibility that it would, many tax experts believe that any introduction of a consumption-based tax should be coupled with an effective inheritance tax.

Transitional Concerns

Any change in the tax law is likely to be accompanied by some transitional costs. Whether a consumption-based tax will have significant transitional costs depends explicitly on the specific type of tax introduced. Therefore an analysis of possible transitional problems will be included in the discussion of each type of consumption tax.

Effect on Stability

Since consumption is more stationary than income, a consumption tax will be less stabilizing than an income tax. However, it is unlikely that a consumption-based tax would become a dominant source of federal revenues in the immediate future, and since the government has many ways to stabilize the economy, this argument does not seem to be a cogent one against a consumption-based tax.

Effect on Labor Supply

For a given level of government receipts, a consumption tax at a flat rate initially may place a greater tax burden on wage income than a broad-based income tax using a flat rate. The reason is that the very wealthy obtain more of their income from nonwage sources than the less wealthy and also consume less of their income. With everything else the same, a flat consumption tax would adversely affect the supply of labor.[14] How adverse the effect would be is an empirical issue. Chapter 3 contains an analysis of the literature on this point, and the conclusion is that the most important adverse effect would be on second wage earners in a household.

Value-Added Taxes

There are many variants of VATs. The particular form of the VAT that is used extensively in Europe emerged as a reform of a system of turnover taxes. If a government were to introduce a VAT as a totally new tax, there is no reason to choose the specific form of the tax as employed in Europe. In comparison with other forms of the VAT, the European method has both advantages and disadvantages.

Conceptually a VAT taxes the value-added by each legal entity in the production and sales chain. The variants of a VAT differ along the following dimensions: the mechanics of calculating the tax liability, the entity that pays the tax (which is not the same thing as who bears the tax), and the treatment of capital expenditures.

The Mechanics

Invoice Method

There are three major ways to calculate the tax liability of a VAT. The method used in Europe is the invoice method. Each legal entity—producer or retailer—adds a percentage to each taxable sale, much as a retailer does under the U.S. sales tax. Except for the sale to the ultimate consumers, the tax is stated separately. In much of Europe, the quoted price to the ultimate consumer includes the VAT and is not separately stated.

Each legal entity is then allowed as a tax credit the taxes that it paid to its suppliers. This tax credit is calculated as the sum of the taxes shown on the invoices of the suppliers; hence the name. The advantage of this system is that it provides an audit trail in the collection of the tax. In addition, except for the final entity that sells the product to the consumer, there is little incentive to misreport taxes. Indeed a legal entity has an incentive to make sure that each invoice of its suppliers is correctly stated.

A conference of European economists sponsored by the Brookings Institution concluded from the limited evidence available that this audit trail was not as useful as theory might suggest.[15] Of course the VAT was introduced into Europe before the wide availability of computers. If it were introduced today, perhaps it could be introduced in such a way as to take full advantage of the audit trail. The benefits of preserving the audit trail would have to be weighed carefully against the costs that the private sector would have to bear to change existing accounting systems and the additional collection costs imposed upon the government.

An obvious disadvantage of the invoice method of determining the tax liability is the cost of the bookkeeping placed on the private sector. In response to this problem, it is common in Europe to exempt small businesses from paying the VAT. In return for this exemption, such businesses are not allowed as a tax credit the VAT paid to their suppliers. In addition, farmers frequently are exempted from the invoice system and are taxed in various ways.

Finally, in order to preserve the progressivity in the tax structure, it is common to levy the VAT at different rates for different commodities based on whether the commodity is deemed a necessity or luxury. Such differential rates obviously distort relative prices. In addition the existence of these multiple rates brings with it the problems of classifying goods and services into distinct categories. These problems, however, are probably no more severe than those faced by those individual states in the United States that impose differential sales taxes or those faced by the U.S. Customs.

In Europe the existence of differential taxes, the exemption of some entities from the system, and the special treatment frequently accorded farmers makes the collection of the VAT extremely cumbersome. Hemming and Kay estimate that the governmental costs in the United Kingdom of collecting the VAT per pound of revenue are of the same order of magnitude as the costs of collecting the corporate tax.[16] Yet to put these costs into perspective, it is important to realize that the costs of collecting the VAT or corporate tax in the UK are somewhat less than the costs of collecting the individual tax on wages and about a third of the costs of collecting the individual tax on self-employed income, rent, and interest.[17]

The Subtraction Method

The subtraction method is similar conceptually to the invoice method but would not require as much bookkeeping. Much like the administration of sales taxes in the United States, the VAT would be collected on each taxable sale, and the tax liability of the legal entity would be calculated on the basis of total sales. The tax credit would be derived from those aggregate expenditure categories on which the VAT would have been paid in prior stages of the production process. Thus a legal entity would not have to keep track of each individual invoice but only those aggregate expenditure categories subject to the same VAT. Alternatively if the VAT were the same percentage for all commodities, the tax liability from the VAT could be calculated as a percentage of sales less allowable expenses.

Probably it would be possible to adapt the reporting requirements demanded under the current U.S. corporate tax to those required by the subtraction method of determining the VAT with relative ease. Except for capital expenditures, the major difference between the calculation of the current corporate tax and the subtraction method is that labor costs and interest expenses on which no VAT is paid would not be deductible.

Addition Method
The addition method adds together those factors that contribute to the value-added by the legal entity. Some of the primary factors that add value are labor expense, interest, and net income. Thus this method would require the calculation of net income, just as under the current corporate tax, and would entail many of the same reporting problems as the current system. We know of no country that has implemented this method of calculating the VAT.

Collection of Tax

There are two methods of collecting the tax: the destination method and the origination method. As far as we know, every country with a VAT uses the destination method. In this method the taxing authority where the ultimate consumer lives receives the tax, whereas in the origination method, the taxing authority where the value is added receives the tax. When a product is produced and consumed within a single country, there is no practical difference between these two methods.

For internationally traded goods the methods are quite different. In a country using the destination method, the government does not collect from an exporter the VAT on the export but still allows a tax credit for the VAT paid by the exporter to its suppliers. In effect the exporter receives a refund of the VAT paid to its suppliers. The importing country using the same method would tax the imported product at its rate for the VAT. Thus all of the tax revenue from the VAT goes to the country in which the ultimate consumption takes place.[18] In contrast a country using the origination method would not rebate the previously paid VAT on exports and would not levy a VAT on imports.

On the surface the destination method would seem to neutralize differences in the levels of government taxation among those countries that use this method. It might also appear that a country that does not have VAT of the destination form, such as the United States, may place its exporting industries at a competitive disadvantage. One would anticipate, however, that in a world of floating exchange rates, the exchange rate itself would tend to change so as to undo this apparent disadvantage, restoring purchasing power parity.

Although exchange rates do tend to move toward purchasing power parity, they can deviate from such parity for extended periods of time. In today's environment high real interest rates may be a more important factor than purchasing power parity in explaining the exchange rate in the United States. If so the introduction of a VAT as a replacement for corporate and other types of taxes may provide a temporary stimulus to exporting firms. Ultimately changes in the exchange rates would be expected to undo this advantage. However, if the VAT were levied at differential rates within a nation, internal relative prices would change, and changes in exchange rates would be unable to neutralize this effect. Thus the competitive position of some industries in world trade would be improved and others hurt.

Capital Expenditures

There are three basic methods of treating capital expenditures under a VAT. The method used in Europe permits an immediate tax credit for the VAT paid on capital expenditures. The second method allows a tax credit for the VAT paid on capital expenditures but amortized over the productive life of the capital. The third method allows no tax credit. Only the method used in Europe results in a true consumption tax.

The method used in Europe is the most favorable to capital expenditures and would be simple to administer. The second and third methods require that a legal entity distinguish between capital and noncapital expenditures. In addition the second method requires an amortization schedule and would therefore be subject to many of the same problems implicit in the current tax system in the United States.

Potential Revenue from a VAT

A VAT has the potential to raise substantial revenues. A VAT of 1 percent applied to half of the goods consumed in the United States would raise in 1985 about $10 billion to $12 billion.[19] Applying the VAT to only half of the potentially taxable consumption goods is based on the assumed political realities that a large fraction of the transactions would not be taxed. This estimate may be subject to large error. Even if it were in error by 25 percent either way, the point still holds that a VAT has the potential to raise substantial revenues. To appreciate the magnitude of this number, a 30 percent VAT applied to half the potentially taxable consumption goods or 15 percent applied to the total would generate in 1985 almost the same amount of revenue as the federal personal income tax. A VAT of 30 percent is well within the range utilized by some European countries.

Incidence

The analysis of the incidence of the current U.S. tax system by income class in chapter 2 assumed that the consumer bore the entire burden of state and local sales taxes, as well as federal excise taxes. In other words the selling prices before sales and excise taxes would be the same with or without such sales and excise taxes. If the same assumption is made for the VAT, any VAT with a flat rate applied uniformly across all consumption goods would be a regressive tax when considered by itself. The reason is that consumption as a percentage of income declines with increases in income; however, a tax should not be judged by itself but rather in the context of all taxes and transfer payments.

Given our conclusion that once transfer payments are taken into account the overall tax structure is slightly progressive, a modest VAT could be implemented without changing the overall tax structure to a regressive one. Nonetheless the resulting overall tax structure would necessarily be less progressive than currently.

Using a VAT to replace a substantial portion of the sums collected by the federal individual income tax would be highly regressive. The European experience, however, indicates that a government has sufficient tools available to undo this regressivity, such as differential rates for the VAT tax and family allowances financed by other taxes. Nevertheless the required steps would be substantial and quite costly in terms of transitional problems and unforeseen consequences.

Transitional Problems

The administrative difficulties and costs of implementing a VAT system depend on the specific form of the VAT. If the VAT were calculated by the subtraction method, the implementation should be fairly straightforward, particularly if the VAT were administered at a flat rate. If the VAT were calculated by the invoice method as in Europe, the costs of implementation could be great, particularly for retailers with many small transactions. Entire accounting systems might have to be redesigned, and the government would need to train and employ additional tax collectors.

A major economic problem of implementing a VAT or any other type of consumption tax is that those individuals who had saved in prior years to provide for future consumption would find that they were taxed twice.[20] They were taxed on the income that they had saved, and then they would be taxed on the consumption provided by these dollars. On balance the younger sector of society would benefit at the expense of the older sector, particularly the retired who are living on their savings. Under current law retired people living on pensions from tax-protected funds are taxed the same as they would be under a VAT.

For a modest VAT some might judge this transfer from the older to the younger sectors of society to be small enough to ignore. Alternatively some might consider that a modest transfer to the younger sectors would offset to some extent the relatively more favorable tax treatment of the older sector in the current law. For instance, older persons receive twice the number of exemptions, receive a portion of their social security without tax, have social security benefits frequently in excess of the actuarial value of their contributions, and have an extremely favorable treatment on any capital gains realized on the sale of their principal residence. If the VAT rate is high or if the transitional costs of even a modest VAT are judged excessive, the government would need to take steps to recompense those individuals who were using savings for consumption, primarily older individuals. Methods to accomplish this goal might include increased exemptions or tax credits to selected groups of taxpayers.

Finally, there is a valid concern that the introduction of a flat rate VAT would be inflationary. The reason is that the CPI as normally calculated would increase by the amount of the VAT, even if the proceeds of the VAT were used to reduce individual income taxes. In this case consumers in the aggregate are no worse off than they were before, so that the observed increase in the CPI is merely cosmetic. However, the costs of contracts or government programs with cost-of-living-adjustment clauses will increase and ultimately lead to real inflation. Although undoubtedly it would be extremely difficult politically, any government that introduced a VAT should try to find some way to make sure that the initial increase in the CPI does not activate these cost clauses. For example, the CPI itself could be replaced with a restated CPI that did not show the initial increase. Alternatively there could be a statute that inactivates all cost clauses for a short period of time or that specifies a maximum allowable percentage.[21]

Some concern has also been expressed that firms will view a VAT as an added cost and will increase their prices by not only the VAT but also by a profit margin applied to the VAT.[22] This concern assumes that firms on balance have an extremely large amount of oligopoly power. In a competitive world there is little basis for this concern, but in a less than competitive world, this concern may have some merit, especially in the short term.

VAT as One Component

The complete replacement of the current income-based tax system with a VAT probably is not politically feasible without substantial institutional changes to preserve overall equity; however, combining a VAT with the current tax system has some appeal. A modest VAT of around 6 percent or 7 percent would raise substantial revenues. These revenues could be used to increase the standard exemptions and zero bracket amounts so as to exempt large numbers of persons now in the lower-income brackets from having to file, to provide family assistance to the lowest-income families, and to lower the marginal tax rates on household income at all levels of income.[23] Such a package has the potential to simplify the process of reporting taxes for lower-income families while maintaining the same tax incidence by income class as under the current system. Alternatively some of the additional revenue from a VAT could be used to narrow the budget deficit.

Sales Tax

A sales tax is a consumption tax that is collected only at the final point of sale to a consumer. Assuming that producers prior to the final retailers do not add a markup to a VAT, both should raise the same amount of revenue and have the same impact on the economy. The principal arguments that have been advanced in favor of a VAT pertain to possible violations of the rights of states that have relied heavily on sales taxes and to the presumption that there would be greater compliance if the tax were collected from more legal entities than merely final retailers.[24] The principal argument in favor of a sales tax is that it can be collected with less administration. The strength of this last argument hinges on the specific form of the VAT that is being considered.

Personal Consumption Tax

A personal consumption tax is collected directly from the taxpayer and is based on the total number of dollars spent on consumption during the tax period, which is the same as income less net saving. Because the tax is collected directly from the taxpayer, the tax schedule could be as progressive as the current income tax schedule. In some versions of a personal consumption tax, imputed consumption or income is included.

Although a taxpayer's consumption in principle could be calculated directly, actual proposals for a personal consumption tax employ an indirect method. A taxpayer's actual consumption in any tax period can be estimated as the difference between the total inflows and those outflows used for nonconsumption purposes. Inflows would include wages, investment receipts, proceeds from sales of investment assets, receipts of gifts and inheritance, and the proceeds of loans. In some versions inflows also include imputed income used for consumption. Since these inflows can be used only for consumption or nonconsumption items, knowing the cash outflows for nonconsumption purposes gives as a residual the taxpayer's consumption. The primary nonconsumption items are purchases of investment assets, insurance, interest paid on loans, payments of gifts and inheritance, and repayments of loans.[25] Readers should note carefully how loans, gifts, and inheritances are treated under a personal consumption tax. Also this indirect method does not require the valuation of unrealized gains and losses on investments, which greatly simplifies the calculation.

If the corporate tax were eliminated or integrated with the consumption tax (which is the same thing under a consumption tax), there is a real possibility that after transitional adjustments have been made, the federal tax code might be vastly simplified. One of the major complexities in the current code system stems from the need to spread one-time expenses over several tax periods or to impute income to more than one tax period. With a consumption tax, all that counts is the taxpayer's net cash flow, possibly adjusted by imputed income. There would be no need for detailed depreciation schedules, rules for calculating capital gains, or most of the detailed record keeping required of the current tax system. Whether the simplification would actually be achieved hinges on the specific way in which a particular consumption tax is defined.

Although once established a consumption tax may have some very desirable properties, there are major transitional problems in moving from the current U.S. tax system to a personal consumption tax. To realize the simplification inherent in such a tax, the current system would have to be abolished and the lost revenues replaced by the consumption tax. Thus a personal consumption tax would represent a major change in the tax structure. Such major changes may be accompanied by possibly great transitional problems and unforeseen consequences.

Description

If one ignores imputed income, primarily the rental value of owner-occupied houses and transitional problems, a consumption tax could be implemented with relative ease. The taxpayer would sum all cash inflows and deduct from that sum all outflows attributable to nonconsumption items. Imputed income from housing and consumer durables would be ignored, and the cost of purchasing housing and consumer durables including interest would not be deductible.[26] A recent issue of the *Economist* presents an example of this approach.[27] The only major unresolved issue is the treatment of gifts and bequests, which is also a problem area, though perhaps not as great, for an income-based tax. Of particular concern is how the donor and recipient treat gifts and bequests for tax purposes. For example, should a donor treat such an item as consumption? How should the recipient treat the gift?

Blueprints notes that a properly constructed consumption-based tax does tax imputed income. The reasoning is as follows: If the consumption tax is flat, it makes no difference when a taxpayer pays the tax on funds that are saved and then used for future consumption. Assume a 30 percent tax and that the taxpayer wishes to invest $100 at 10 percent for twenty years. If the taxpayer is permitted a current deduction for the $100, he or she will pay no current tax and is able to invest the full amount. At the end of twenty years the $100 will have grown to $672.75, which after a tax of 30 percent would give $470.93 for consumption. Alternatively if the taxpayer paid the tax at the beginning, he or she would have only $70 to invest. At the end of twenty years this $70 would have grown to $470.93, exactly the same as if the tax were postponed. Note that in both cases, there is no tax on the interest income.

To implement a consumption-based tax, *Blueprints* proposes that investments be classified as either qualified or prepaid. A taxpayer placing funds in a qualified investment would receive an immediate deduction of the value of the investment from his or her tax base. At some subsequent date the withdrawal of the proceeds of the investment would be included in the taxpayer's tax base. This procedure is similar to the way in which IRAs are treated by the tax law currently. Thus the institutional arrangements for handling such investments are already available, making this part of the plan easy to implement.

A prepaid investment is one for which no current deduction is allowed, so that such an investment would come from after-tax dollars. Under a consumption tax there would be no tax on the total investment income from prepaid investments.[28] The taxpayer would be free to consume the investment at any point without including the expenditure in his or her tax base.

Now let us see how these two types of accounts tax the imputed rental value of owner-occupied housing. Assume that owner-occupied housing can be classified only as a prepaid investment and that the taxpayer uses only wage income in the current period to buy a home. Since he or she would not be allowed a deduction for the investment in the house, the taxpayer would in effect be paying a tax on this investment. If the price of a house represents the discounted value of the future imputed rent, the taxpayer has paid tax on the consumption of the imputed rent.

Now consider a taxpayer who takes out a mortgage of $80,000 to buy a $100,000 house. Let us examine the tax treatment of the down payment of $20,000. If the down payment came from current wage income or from previously prepaid investments, the taxpayer ultimately would pay or would have already paid a tax on the down payment. If the taxpayer withdraws the $20,000 from a qualified investment, he or she would have to recognize this withdrawal in his or her tax base. The investor has the choice of recognizing the $80,000 mortgage in his or her tax base or of not recognizing it. Most home owners probably would elect not to recognize the mortgage and avoid the immediate payment of the tax. In this case the repayment of the mortgage with the associated interest payments

would not be deductible and thus would be paid with prepaid dollars. As a result the taxpayer has paid in taxes the
same percentage of the present value of the house as if he
or she had purchased the house with no mortgage.

The other alternative open to the taxpayer is to include
the mortgage in his or her current tax base. In this case he
or she will pay the full consumption tax on the house immediately since the house can be treated only as a prepaid
investment; however, the interest and mortgage payments
will be allowed as deductions. Again, the present value of
the tax liability is the same. The only difference is the timing of the tax payments.

In conformity with a tax on consumption alone, *Blueprints* would allow the donor to deduct gifts and bequests
from his or her tax base and would require that such gifts
be included in the tax base of the recipient. To see how this
might work, assume that a parent died with $500,000 in a
qualified investment. The estate would have to withdraw
the $500,000 before giving it to the heirs. The first transac-
tion increases the tax base of the donor, while the second
decreases it, so that the donor pays no tax.[29] The heir
would have to recognize $500,000 as income. To avoid the
resulting tax, the heir probably would place most of the
funds in a qualified investment. The overall effect is that
no tax is paid at death by the donor or the donee.

The Committee on Simplification, Section of Taxation,
the American Bar Association, has analyzed with great
care this particular proposal for a personal consumption
tax.[30] Their conclusion is that this proposal would simplify
the tax structure in some ways, particularly with respect
to depreciation and the like; however, the presence of
two types of investment, qualified and prepaid, is likely to
lead to abuses and complications. They construct one tax
shelter that is implementable under the specific proposal
contained in *Blueprints*. Although the proposal could be

changed to eliminate the possibility of this one technique, they point out that it is highly likely that other ways will be found to use the two types of assets for tax avoidance.[31] Their overall conclusion is that *Blueprints'* proposed consumption tax would not lead to the simplification that is promised.

Potential Revenues

A personal consumption tax would have the potential to raise the same amount of revenue as the current individual income tax. For 1976 *Blueprints* estimated that the taxable income before exemptions under the law at that time was $817.9 billion. In contrast the taxable amount under their consumption tax before exemptions was $1,135.6 billion.[32] The difference between the two taxable amounts is due to deductions and income exclusions present in the existing tax code, such as the favorable treatment of capital gains and the exclusion of municipal bond interest, that *Blueprints* proposes to eliminate. If political realities permit eliminating these deductions and exclusions, the tax base for a personal consumption tax would be greater than that for the current income tax but not as great as that for the broad-based income taxes discussed in chapters 4 and 5.

For a joint return, *Blueprints* proposes the following tax rates for a consumption tax: a marginal tax rate of 10 percent in the $0–5,200 income bracket, 28 percent in the $5,200–30,000 bracket, and 40 percent in the over $30,000 bracket. Each return would have a basic exemption of $1,500 and $800 per taxpayer and dependent. Thus the marginal tax rates are less than under current law at that time but are greater than those that would occur under the broader-based income tax codes now under discussion.

Incidence

The analyses in *Blueprints* and in other sources show that a personal consumption-based tax can be devised that would collect the same amount of revenue by consumption groups as under the current law.[33] Of course, within any consumption group, some will be paying greater tax and some less, depending on the extent to which the taxpayer currently receives income that can be excluded under current law and takes advantage of deductions that would effectively be eliminated under a consumption-based tax.

Transition Costs

The two primary reasons for moving to a personal consumption tax are the possible simplification of the tax system and the removal of some of the distortions introduced into the saving and investment process by an income-based tax. The possible simplification of the tax system would require the complete elimination of the current income-based tax system at both the individual and corporate level and its replacement with a personal consumption tax and, possibly in addition, a corporate cash-flow tax. Thus to realize the advantages of simplification, there would have to be major changes in the tax law. Such major changes undoubtedly would have both significant foreseen and unforeseen costs, and indeed *Blueprints* recognizes the existence of this problem.

A major decision about the transition concerns the treatment of individual wealth on which tax has already been paid and unrealized income, such as unrealized capital gains, for which there is an accrued tax liability. Savings held in pension plans present no transitional problems since they are already taxed in the same way that they would be under the proposed tax. Almost any transitional set of rules will give some taxpayers windfall gains and some windfall losses. The goal is to find some transitional set of rules to minimize these gains and losses.

Blueprints proposes the following transitional scheme. Existing wealth on which taxes have already been paid would be classified as prepaid assets.[34] Since subsequent dividends and interest no longer would be taxable, one would expect a one-time gain for holders of these types of assets. To mitigate this gain, *Blueprints* proposes that taxpayers calculate their tax under the old system and the new system for ten years and pay the maximum of the two taxes.[35]

Blueprints explores the possibility of having all taxpayers realize their unrealized gains and losses at the initiation of the new system but concludes, "This is not administratively attractive, so for ten years all capital gains would be taxed on realization, whichever tax base the individual was using."[36] At the end of the ten-year adjustment period, all remaining gains and losses that were accrued at the initiation of the new system and not yet realized would be taxed.[37] Finally the corporate tax would be retained for ten years and then abolished. *Blueprints* provides no data on the present value of the potential revenue loss.

The advantage of this set of transition rules is that those who have accumulated assets in after-tax dollars are not then taxed again on the consumption of these assets. Moreover unrealized gains and losses do not escape taxation. It should be noted that this transition scheme requires the existence of qualified assets and prepaid assets and that some households with substantial assets may not have to pay much tax for a long period of time.

In sum, both the foreseen and unforeseen transitional costs of replacing the current personal and corporate income tax with a personal consumption tax are likely to be large. To realize the simplification possibilities of a consumption tax, these costs would have to be borne. If the goal is not simplification but instead the removal of incentives to consume early in life rather than save and to remove the distortions in the investment process caused by the inability of any set of regulations to allocate correctly expenses and income to tax periods, another approach is available.

IRAs are taxed almost as they would be under a consumption-based tax and thus could provide some of the economic benefits of a consumption tax with perhaps fewer transitional costs.[38] The major difference is the penalty for early withdrawal and the limitation on the amount of the yearly contribution. To utilize IRAs as a model in a consumption-based tax scheme, the penalty for early withdrawal would have to be eliminated; however, rather than eliminating the annual limitation on contributions, it might be desirable to maintain some limit so as to avoid excessive concentration of wealth.[39] Expanding the role of IRAs moves the tax system in the opposite direction from that espoused by those who wish to broaden the tax base. Furthermore maintaining the same degree of progressivity may require changes in other parts of the tax code.

We make no recommendation as to whether the tax system should move in the direction of a consumption-based or an income-based tax system, but indicate the strengths and weaknesses of different approaches to the reform of our current tax system.

Appendix A:
Detailed Comparison
of Tax Expenditure
Estimates

The table in this appendix shows the correspondence between items in the Joint Committee on Taxation–Congressional Budget Office estimates of the tax expenditures and items being modified in the Bradley-Gephardt proposal for tax reform as far as possible so as to facilitate a construction of rough estimates of revenue impacts of all items in the Bradley-Gephardt proposal. The initial identification of the correspondence was attempted using a document entitled "Explanation of the 'Fair Tax Act of 1983' " provided by Senator Bradley's office. We have subsequently checked with various experts as well as with a representative of the senator's office concerning cases that were unclear to us, and we believe that our interpretations are basically accurate, although it is still possible that the table contains a few minor errors of identification.

In computing remaining tax expenditures and revenue recoveries, we have followed the following general procedure:

1. When an item that is excluded from the tax base is retained, the entire estimated amount by JTC-CBO is transferred to the column "remaining tax expenditures."

2. When an item is repealed outright, the entire estimated amount by JTC-CBO is transferred to the column "revenue recoveries."

3. When an item that is a deduction from the tax base is retained, in the case of corporations the entire estimated amount by JTC-CBO is transferred to the column "remaining tax expenditures." In the case of individuals we have adopted the following approximation. First, we take the 1983 tax table for married persons filing joint returns (of total itemized deductions, joint returns account for more than four-fifths of the total in terms of dollar amount in recent years). Next we take the distribution of the dollar amount of deduction of an item by adjusted gross income shown in the statistics of income for individuals closest to the item in question. We then compute the weighted average of the rates shown in the tax table using the distribution referred to above as weights. The result is what we refer to as weighted average of applicable marginal rates. This is computed for each item separately because weights vary from item to item. Once these weighted averages are computed, the JTC-CBO estimate of the tax expenditure is multiplied by the ratio of 0.14 to the applicable average of marginal rates, and the result is entered in the column "remaining tax expenditures." The difference between this figure and the original tax expenditure estimate is then entered in the column "revenue recoveries." Note that these weights are taken from statistics of income for 1981, since these are the latest figures available.

For a few items in the Bradley-Gephardt proposal we could not estimate revenue impacts. In some cases they are very small items for which JTC-CBO have not estimated the amount of tax expenditure; in others the provision involves a change whose impacts can be estimated through the use of a very different set of data, even then with a very large margin of error. We have not been able to carry out all possible inquiries but believe that those remaining items that we did not prepare an estimate of revenue impacts for are quite small and will not materially affect our results.

Detailed Comparison of Tax Expenditure Estimates by Joint Committee on Taxation and Congressional Budget Office with Provisions of the Bradley-Gephardt Proposal (millions of dollars, fiscal year 1983)

Function and subfunction	JCT-CBO estimates Corp.	JCT-CBO estimates Indiv.	Disposition by B-G proposal[a]	Remaining tax expenditure Corp.	Remaining tax expenditure Indiv.	Revenue recovery Corp.	Revenue recovery Indiv.	Applicable weighted average of marginal rates[b]
050 NATIONAL DEFENSE.								
051 Department of Defense—Military								
(a) Exclusion of benefits and allowances to armed forces personnel		2,205	Retained		2,205			
(b) Exclusion of military disability pensions		165	Retained		165			
150 INTERNATIONAL AFFAIRS								
155 International finance programs								
(a) Exclusion of income earned abroad by U.S. citizens		1,285	Repealed				1,285	
(b) Deferral of income of domestic international sales corporations	1,390		Repealed			1,390		
(c) Deferral of income of controlled foreign corporations	430		Repealed			430		
250 GENERAL SCIENCE, SPACE, AND TECHNOLOGY								
251 General science and basic research								
(a) Expensing of research and development expenditures	2165	105	Retained	2,165	105			
(b) Credit for increasing research activities	615	30	Repealed			615	30	

Detailed Comparison of Tax Expenditure Estimates by Joint Committee on Taxation and Congressional Budget Office with Provisions of the Bradley-Gephardt Proposal (millions of dollars, fiscal year 1983), *continued*

Function and subfunction	JCT-CBO estimates Corp.	JCT-CBO estimates Indiv.	Disposition by B-G proposal[a]	Remaining tax expenditure Corp.	Remaining tax expenditure Indiv.	Revenue recovery Corp.	Revenue recovery Indiv.	Applicable weighted average of marginal rates[b]
(c) Suspension of regulations relating to allocation under section 861 of research and experimental expenditures	120		Retained	120				
270 ENERGY								
271 *Energy supply*								
(a) Expensing of exploration and development costs								
Oil and gas	660	875	Repealed			660	875	
Other fuels	30		Repealed			30		
(b) Excess of percentage over cost depletion								
Oil and gas	375	1,425	Repealed			375	1,425	
Other fuels	325	15	Repealed			325	15	
(c) Capital gains treatment of royalties from coal	35	140	Eliminated as part of capital gain			35	140	
(d) Alternative fuel production credit	5		Repealed			5		
(e) Alcohol fuel credit	5		Repealed			5		
(f) Exclusion of interest on state and local government industrial development bonds for energy production facilities	15	5	Repealed			15	5	

No.	Item			Treatment		
(g)	Alternative conservation and new technology credits — Supply incentives		340	Repealed		340
(h)	Residential energy credits — Supply incentives	215	10	Repealed	215	10
272	*Energy conservation*					
(a)	Residential energy credits — Conservation incentives		330	Repealed		330
(b)	Alternative conservation and new technology credits — Conservation incentives	135	[b]	Repealed	135	5
(c)	Energy credit for intercity buses	5		Repealed	5	
300	NATURAL RESOURCES AND ENVIRONMENT					
302	*Conservation and land management*					
(a)	Capital gains treatment of certain timber income	275	95	Eliminated as part of capital gain	275	95
(b)	Investment credit and seven-year amortization for reforestation expenditures		10	Repealed		10
303	*Recreational resources*					
(a)	Tax incentives for preservation of historic structures	65	130	Repealed	65	130
304	*Pollution control and abatement*					
(a)	Exclusion of interest on state and local government pollution control bonds	900	440	Repealed	900	440

Detailed Comparison of Tax Expenditure Estimates by Joint Committee on Taxation and Congressional Budget Office with Provisions of the Bradley-Gephardt Proposal (millions of dollars, fiscal year 1983), *continued*

Function and subfunction	JCT-CBO estimates Corp.	Indiv.	Disposition by B-G proposal[a]	Remaining tax expenditure Corp.	Indiv.	Revenue recovery Corp.	Indiv.	Applicable weighted average of marginal rates[b]
(b) Exclusion of payments in aid of construction of water, sewage, gas, and electric utilities	45	b	Retained	45				
306 *Other natural resources*								
(a) Expensing of exploration and development costs, nonfuel minerals	55	b	Repealed			55		
(b) Excess of percentage over cost depletion, nonfuel minerals	270	10	Repealed			270	10	
(c) Capital gains treatment of iron ore	5	5	Eliminated as part of capital gain			5	5	
350 AGRICULTURE								
351 *Farm income stabilization* (n. 1)								
(a) Expensing of certain capital outlays	85	475		85	475			
(b) Capital gains treatment of certain income	30	455	Eliminated as part of capital gain			30	455	
(c) Deductibility of patronage dividends and certain other items of cooperatives	950	−390	Retained	950	−390			
(d) Exclusion of certain cost-sharing payments		50	Retained		50			

370 COMMERCE AND HOUSING CREDIT

371 Mortgage credit and thrift insurance

		Amount	Treatment				
(a)	Excess bad debt reserves of financial institutions	335	Repealed		335		
(b)	Deductibility of mortgage interest on owner-occupied homes	25,065	Retained at 14%	12,142	12,923		(0.289)
(c)	Deductibility of property tax on owner-occupied homes	8,765	Retained at 14%	4,104	4,661		(0.299)
(d)	Exclusion of interest on state and local government housing bonds for owner-occupied housing	1,060	Repealed	450	1,060	450	
(e)	Exclusion of interest on state and local government housing bonds for rental housing	585	Repealed	285	585	285	
(f)	Deferral of capital gains on home sales	3,770	Retained	3,770			
(g)	Exclusion of capital gains on home sales for persons age 55 and over	1,255	Retained at 14%	608	647		(0.289)

376 Other advancement and regulation of commerce

		Amount	Treatment			
(a)	Exclusion of interest on state and local industrial development bonds	2,355	Repealed	570	2,355	570
(b)	Exemption of credit union income	170	Repealed		170	
(c)	Exclusion of interest on life insurance savings	4,805	Repealed			4,805

Detailed Comparison of Tax Expenditure Estimates by Joint Committee on Taxation and Congressional Budget Office with Provisions of the Bradley-Gephardt Proposal (millions of dollars, fiscal year 1983), *continued*

Function and subfunction	JCT-CBO estimates Corp.	JCT-CBO estimates Indiv.	Disposition by B-G proposal[a]	Remaining tax expenditure Corp.	Remaining tax expenditure Indiv.	Revenue recovery Corp.	Revenue recovery Indiv.	Applicable weighted average of marginal rates[a]
(d) Deductibility of nonmortgage interest in excess of investment income		7,735	Repealed				7,735	
(e) Expensing of construction period interest and taxes	505	275	Repealed			505	275	
(f) Depreciation on rental housing in excess of straight-line (n. 2)	120	575	Modified			120	575	
(g) Depreciation on buildings (other than rental housing) in excess of straight-line (n. 2)	175	150	Modified			175	150	
(h) Reinvestment of dividends in stock of public utilities		365	Repealed				365	
(i) Net interest exclusion			Repealed					
(j) Exclusion of interest on certain savings certificates		2,335	Retained		2,335			
(k) Accelerated depreciation on equipment other than leased property (n. 3)	9,510	1,015	Modified			9,510	1,015	
(l) Safe-harbor leasing	1,745							
Accelerated depreciation and deferral								
(m) Investment credit	1,625							

Item	Description					
(n)	Amortization of business start-up costs	15	105			
(o)	Capital gains other than agriculture, timber, iron ore, and coal	1,770	14,955	Repealed	1,770	14,955
(p)	Capital gains at death	3,975		Retained	3,975	
(q)	Dividend exclusion	445		Repealed		445
(r)	Reduced rates on the first $100,000 of corporate income	5,690		Repealed	5,690	
(s)	Investment credit, other than for employee stock ownership plans (ESOPs), rehabilitation of structures, reforestation and leasing	9,965	3,220	Repealed	9,965	3,220
400	**TRANSPORTATION**					
401	*Ground transportation*					
(a)	Amortization of motor-carrier operating rights	70	5	Retained	70	5
(b)	Exclusion of interest on state and local government mass transit bonds	45	15	Retained	45	15
403	*Water transportation*					
(a)	Deferral of tax on shipping companies	30		Retained		30
450	**COMMUNITY AND REGIONAL DEVELOPMENT**					
451	*Community development*					
(a)	Five-year amortization for housing rehabilitation	20	30	Repealed	20	30

Detailed Comparison of Tax Expenditure Estimates by Joint Committee on Taxation and Congressional Budget Office with Provisions of the Bradley-Gephardt Proposal (millions of dollars, fiscal year 1983), *continued*

Function and subfunction	JCT-CBO estimates Corp.	JCT-CBO estimates Indiv.	Disposition by B-G proposal[a]	Remaining tax expenditure Corp.	Remaining tax expenditure Indiv.	Revenue recovery Corp.	Revenue recovery Indiv.	Applicable weighted average of marginal rates[b]
(b) Investment credit for rehabilitation of structures other than historic structures	175	160	Repealed			175	160	
500 EDUCATION, TRAINING, EMPLOYMENT AND SOCIAL SERVICES								
502 *Higher education*								
(a) Exclusion of scholarship and fellowship income		415	Repealed in excess of tuition					
(b) Employer educational assistance		40	Repealed				40	
(c) Exclusion of interest on state and local government student loan bonds	150	70	Repealed			150	70	
(d) Parental personal exemption for students age 19 or over		995	Retained at 14%		696		229	(2.00)
(e) Deductibility of charitable contributions (education)	280	495	½ for corporation, retained for individual	140	219	140	276	(316)
504 *Training and employment services*								
(a) Credit for child and dependent care expenses		1,520	Modified		1,064		456	(200)

			Status				
(b) Targeted jobs credit	215	75	Retained	215	75		
505 Other labor services							
(a) Exclusion of employee meals and lodging (other than military)		680	Retained		680		
(b) Tax credit for employee stock ownership plans (ESOPs)	1,250		Repealed	1,250			
(c) Exclusion for employer-provided child care		10	Repealed		10		
506 Social services							
(a) Deductibility of charitable contributions, other than education and health	350	6,795	½ for corporation, retained for individual	175	3,010	175	(0.316)
(b) Exclusion of contributions to prepaid legal services plans		25	Repealed		25		
(c) Deduction for two-earner married couples		3,555	Repealed		3,555		
(d) Deduction for adoption expenses		10	Repealed		10		
550 HEALTH							
551 Health care services							
(a) Exclusion of employer contributions for medical insurance premiums and medical care		18,645	Repealed		18,645		
(b) Deductibility of medical expenses (n. 4)		3,105	Only in excess of 10 percent of AGI is allowed		3,105		

Detailed Comparison of Tax Expenditure Estimates by Joint Committee on Taxation and Congressional Budget Office with Provisions of the Bradley-Gephardt Proposal (millions of dollars, fiscal year 1983), *continued*

Function and subfunction	JCT-CBO estimates		Disposition by B-G proposal[a]	Remaining tax expenditure		Revenue recovery		Applicable weighted average of marginal rates[b]
	Corp.	Indiv.		Corp.	Indiv.	Corp.	Indiv.	
(c) Exclusion of interest on state and local government hospital bonds	795	385	Repealed				385	
(d) Deductibility of charitable contributions (health)	175	995	½ for corporation, retained for individual	87	441	87	554	(0.316)
(e) Tax credit for orphan drug research	10		Repealed				10	
600 INCOME SECURITY								
601 *General retirement and disability insurance*								
(a) Exclusion of social security benefits								
Disability insurance benefits		1,690	Retained		1,690			
OASI benefits for retired workers		15,685	Retained		15,685			
Benefits for dependents and survivors		3,765	Retained		3,765			
(b) Exclusion of railroad retirement system benefits (n. 5)		780	Modified		500		280	
(c) Exclusion of workmen's compensation benefits		1,870	Retained		1,870			
(d) Exclusion of special benefits for disabled coal miners		170	Retained		170			

(e) Exclusion of disability pay	145	Repealed		145	
601 *General retirement and disability insurance (continued)*					
(a) Net exclusion of pension contributions and earnings					
Employer plans (n. 6)	49,700	Retained	49,700		
(b) Plans for self-employed	1,065	Retained	1,065		
(c) Individual retirement plans	2,695	Retained	2,695		
(d) Exclusion of other employee benefits					
Premiums on group term life insurance	2,100	Repealed		2,100	
(e) Premiums on accident and disability insurance	115	Repealed		115	
(f) Additional exemption for the blind	35	Retained	35		(0.140)
(g) Additional exemption for the elderly	2,365	Retained	1,656	709	(0.200)
(h) Tax credit for the elderly	135	Repealed		135	
603 *Unemployment compensation*					
Exclusion of untaxed unemployment insurance benefits	3,260	Repealed		3,260	
609 *Other income security* (n. 7)					
(a) Exclusion of public assistance benefits	430	Retained	430		
(b) Deductibility of casualty and theft losses	575	Retained	575		
(c) Earned income credit[d]	385				

Detailed Comparison of Tax Expenditure Estimates by Joint Committee on Taxation and Congressional Budget Office with Provisions of the Bradley-Gephardt Proposal (millions of dollars, fiscal year 1983), *continued*

Function and subfunction	JCT-CBO estimates Corp.	JCT-CBO estimates Indiv.	Disposition by B-G proposal[a]	Remaining tax expenditure Corp.	Remaining tax expenditure Indiv.	Revenue recovery Corp.	Revenue recovery Indiv.	Applicable weighted average of marginal rates[b]
700 VETERANS' BENEFITS AND SERVICES								
701 *Income security for veterans*								
(a) Exclusion of veterans' disability compensation		1,820	Retained		1,820			
(b) Exclusion of veterans' pensions		310	Retained		310			
702 *Veterans' education, training, and rehabilitation*								
Exclusion of GI bill benefits		130	Retained		130			
800 GENERAL GOVERNMENT								
806 *Other general government credits and deductions for political contributions*		190	Repealed				190	
850 GENERAL PURPOSE FISCAL ASSISTANCE								
851 *General revenue sharing*								
(a) Exclusion of interest on general purpose state and local debt	6,985	3,435	Retained	6,985	3,435			
(b) Deductibility of nonbusiness state and local taxes (other than on owner-occupied homes)		20,060	Other than income repealed		6,012		14,048	(0.337)
852 *Other general purpose fiscal assistance*								

Tax credit for corporations receiving income from doing business in United States possessions	1,350	Repealed				1,350
900 INTEREST						
901 Interest on the public debt						
Deferral of interest on savings bonds		50	Retained			50
Grand total*	56,710	239,319	11,113	127,727	43,822	110,373

*The sums of remaining tax expenditures and revenue recoveries do not equal the original JTC-CBO estimates because we have been unable to allocate scholarship and fellowship income between tuition and the amount in excess of tuition.

a. Numbers in parentheses refer to corresponding numbered items in the document released by Senator Bradley's office entitled "Explanation of the Fair Tax Act of 1983."

b. For the explanation of this item, see note 8 at the end of this table.

Note 1: Some part of this item is being eliminated but the amount is difficult to estimate. See item F(7) of Senator Bradley's fact sheet.

Note 2: The Bradley-Gephardt proposal attempts to approximate economic depreciation through a fixed schedule. If it succeeds, it would reduce these tax exemptions to zero. However, there is a problem; their tables (see item B in fact sheet) assume a 6 percent inflation rate, while JTC and CBO assume zero inflation in their estimates of tax expenditures. If the inflation rate is in fact less than 6 percent, there may remain some tax expenditures in these items.

Note 3: The safe-harbor leasing provision was replaced by a finance leasing provision by the 1982 modification of the tax code. The Bradley-Gephardt proposal's item 20 is designed to eliminate the remaining part of the safe-harbor leasing provision.

Note 4: We cannot estimate what would remain after the 10 percent limit and then 14 percent is applied to it, but we believe that the remainder will be quite small.

Note 5: We do not know exactly what is the tier II benefit portion of the total; figures entered are estimated.

Note 6: The limits on qualified pension plans are being reduced by one-third. The net effect is hard to estimate, but the effect is small compared to the total of this item. See item F(5) on the fact sheet.

Note 7: This item has become limited to the amount above a certain sum; the Bradley-Gephardt proposal retains the modified version.

Note 8: Figures reported in this column are effective rates at which the item in question was deducted from AGI in arriving at the taxable income in 1981; this information was extracted from The Statistics of Income, Individual Returns (1981). When a particular item was retained under the Bradley-Gephardt proposal, the deduction was allowed at 14 percent, rather than at the effective rate in force in 1981. We have allocated total tax expenditure between the retained part and the recovered part according to this information.

Appendix B: Estimation of the Total Revenue Effects of the Bradley-Gephardt Proposal

Estimation of the total revenue effects of the Bradley-Gephardt proposal is extremely complex. It is especially difficult now because there was a major change in the federal income tax system between 1981 and 1983. For the purposes of policy discussions, our estimates must refer at the earliest to 1983, and preferably to later years, while the latest data available to us are for 1981. Generally basing our conclusions about 1983 on 1981 data is not an insurmountable task because most of the details move in a more or less predictable manner from one year to the next, but this is not the case when such a large change in the tax system has taken place. Thus any computation presented here is subject to an unusual degree of uncertainty, and all must be reviewed and checked further as new information becomes available.

Changes in the Treatment of Personal Exemption

For calendar year 1981 aproximately 49.7 million single returns and 45.7 million joint returns were filed. Thus the total amount of additional exemption provided in the B-G proposal (in which $600 more is given to the taxpayer and his or her spouse but not to other dependents) is

$600 \times 49,700,000 + \$1,200 \times 45,700,000 = \$84.6$ billion.

The total exemption taken in 1981 (the dollar amount) was $231.1 billion. For calendar year 1981 the appropriately weighted average of marginal rates applicable to personal exemption was about 20 percent; between 1981 and 1983 the marginal tax rate should fall by roughly 20 percent, making the equivalent marginal rate close to 16 percent. Since the population has grown at about 1 percent per year for these years, it would not be too far off to estimate the revenue loss due to the presence of personal exemptions under the present tax code as follows:

$231.1 billion $\times$ 1.02 $\times$ 0.16 = $37.7 billion,

while the revenue loss under Bradley-Gephardt is

($231.1 billion + $84.6 billion) $\times$ 1.02 $\times$ 0.14
$$= \$45.1 \text{ billion.}$$

Thus the net loss due to the change in the treatment of personal exemptions under the B-G proposal is roughly $7.4 billion.

Effects of Base-Broadening Measures

The effects were analyzed in as much detail as possible in appendix A. The total effect was estimated to be the net gain in revenue of approximately $110 billion using the 1981 tax rates under the current code.

Effects of Change in Rate Schedule and the Standard Deductions

We need some information on the size distribution of taxable income for 1983 and effective average tax rates applicable to each income class under the current tax code and under the B-G proposal. Note that the definition of taxable income under the current code includes income in the so-called zero bracket; this is the reason why the effects of the change in the rate schedule and of changes in the standard deduction amounts are more easily estimated jointly.

For this purpose, we have first taken the size distribution of adjusted gross income in 1981 from *Statistics of Income for Individuals* and shifted the distribution up so that the total value of the adjusted gross income is moved up in the same proportion as the ratio of 1983 personal income in the national income account to 1981 personal income. We then assumed that the ratio of taxable income to the adjusted gross income in each detailed adjusted gross income class remained the same from 1981 to 1983, and we constructed the size distribution of taxable income for 1983.

We have the effective average tax rate (tax liability after credit/taxable income) in each income class from *Statistics of Income for Individuals* for 1981. In order to obtain the effective average tax rate for 1983, we computed the effective average tax rate schedule implied by the table for taxpayers filing joint returns for 1981 and 1983 (they account for more than 73 percent of the total taxes paid) and computed the ratio between them. The result is shown in table B.1. The 1983 rates are almost roughly 80 percent of 1981 rates, although there is some indication that the top bracket rate declined slightly more than average. (It should be remembered that the top bracket rate was reduced from 70 percent to 50 percent all at once in 1981, while rates for lower-income classes were reduced gradually over three years. Thus the top rate for 1981 already reflects the full effect of the Reagan tax cut, while others do not.) On the strength of this evidence we have approximated 1983 effective average tax rates on taxable income by taking 80 percent of the corresponding rates for 1981. When this schedule of rates is applied to our size distribution of tax-

Table B.1
Effective average tax rate on taxable income at bracket change points,
for married couples filing joint returns, Form 1040

Income (thousands)	1981 effective average rate	1983 effective average rate	Ratio of 1983 to 1981 rate
$ 3.4	0.0%	0.0%	
5.5	5.3	4.2	0.7925
7.6	8.3	6.6	0.7952
11.9	11.8	9.7	0.8220
16.0	14.2	11.5	0.8190
20.2	16.2	13.1	0.8090
24.6	18.3	14.9	0.8142
29.9	20.7	16.8	0.8120
35.2	23.2	18.8	0.8103
45.8	27.8	22.6	0.8130
60.0	32.8	26.7	0.8140
85.6	39.1	31.9	0.8159
109.4	43.5	35.4	0.8140
162.4	50.2	40.1	0.7990
215.4	54.5	42.6	0.7817

able income, the total estimated is $282.6 billion. We have
no direct information on the total tax liability for 1983 at
this time; however, the *President's Economic Report* of February 1984 reports that federal personal tax and nontax receipts for 1981 were $298.6 billion and for 1983 $295.8
billion; revenues from this source were approximately the
same for these two years. Although the concept of the
personal income tax in the national income accounts and
the tax liability in *Statistics of Income* are not the same, they
must move roughly together. According to *Statistics of Income*, the tax liability after credits for 1981 was $282.3 bil-
lion. Thus our estimates for the total tax liability for 1983
are approximately the same as the actual report for 1981. In
view of the evidence from national income accounts, we
believe that our estimates of the size distribution of taxable
income and effective average tax rates for each income
class are approximately correct.

We must now construct an estimated schedule of effective average tax rates on taxable income according to the B-G proposal, keeping in mind that the definition of taxable income we must work with includes the zero bracket amount (standard deduction). Using the rate schedule given in Bradley-Gephardt and the proposed standard deduction amounts for single and joint returns and taking into consideration the fact that weights of single returns are fairly high for low-income classes and then gradually decline, we have constructed estimates for such a schedule, reported in table B.2.

Although both the current rate schedule and the schedule according to the B-G proposal are rough approximations, the general pattern is useful. The B-G rate reduction plus the proposed increase in the standard deduction will benefit very low-income families and also the top income families, especially those whose adjusted gross income is $100,000 or more. For those above $500,000, the program will reduce the effective rate by 35 percent, while for middle-income families, between $13,000 and $50,000, the program will reduce their effective tax rates by only a little more than 20 percent. This reduction in the progressivity of the tax system presumably will be offset by the progressivity-increasing features of the base-broadening provisions. It is still possible, even probable, that the B-G proposal as a whole would tend to favor both ends of income distribution against the middle-income classes.

Using these effective rates and the distribution of taxable income referred to, we conclude that the potential revenue under the B-G proposal for 1983 without their tax-broadening measures would be roughly $210.4 billion; the revenue loss due to the rate deduction and the increase in the standard deductions will be approximately $72 billion.

These changes, being large, generate sizable second-order effects that must be taken into account. There is a minor complication in doing so; in appendix A, in the case

Table B.2
Comparison of effective rates on taxable income by income class, under
current code and B-G proposal, 1983

Gross adjusted income class (thousands)	Average taxable income	Effective average tax rates		Ratio of B-G proposal rates to current rates
		Current code	B-G proposal	
$ 0–1	0.0	0.0%	0.0%	
1–2	2.7	2.0	0.0	
2–3	3.5	3.7	0.0	
3–4	2.7	1.9	0.0	
4–5	3.4	3.7	0.0	
5–6	4.3	5.4	2.6	0.48
6–7	5.2	6.6	3.9	0.59
7–8	6.0	7.1	4.4	0.61
8–9	6.6	7.4	5.5	0.74
9–10	7.4	8.2	6.0	0.73
10–11	8.2	8.9	6.5	0.72
11–12	9.1	9.5	7.0	0.73
12–13	10.0	10.0	7.6	0.76
13–14	10.9	10.5	8.2	0.78
14–15	11.7	10.8	8.9	0.82
15–20	14.1	11.8	9.6	0.81
20–25	18.2	13.2	10.4	0.79
25–30	22.2	14.3	11.2	0.78
30–40	28.0	16.1	12.4	0.76
40–50	35.8	18.7	14.0	0.75
50–75	47.0	22.1	15.8	0.71
75–100	67.7	26.8	19.5	0.73
100–200	103.8	31.8	23.1	0.72
200–500	222.1	38.1	26.8	0.70
500–1,000	494.0	42.6	28.5	0.66
1,000 and more	1632.2	45.9	29.5	0.64

of deductions retained under the B-G proposal, we have already taken the proposed change that these items are deducted only for regular tax computations. Taking this adjustment into consideration, the second-order effect is estimated to be a roughly $20 billion loss:

Base-broadening measures	+ $110 billion
Rate reductions and increased standard deductions	− $ 72 billion
Second-order effects	− $ 20 billion
Net loss due to exemption increase	− $ 7 billion
Total Net Effects	+ $ 11 billion

Thus, our conclusion is that the Bradley-Gephardt proposal is likely to result in the net gain in revenue from the individual income tax system of roughly $11 billion. Our calculations are extremely approximate, and our result should be understood to confirm roughly the statements by sponsors of the proposal that its total revenue effects in the individual income tax system are approximately neutral. In particular in computing the second-order effects, we have taken the simplest linear approximation and probably underestimated the size of the second-order effect, especially if the tax broadening has proportionately more effect at the upper-income classes where the reduction in rates is greater than elsewhere. If this is so, the net total effect can easily be a relatively small revenue loss rather than a relatively small revenue gain.

Notes

Chapter 2

1. The profits of the Federal Reserve System that are returned to the federal government and are considered a tax in the national income accounts are excluded in determining these percentages. In addition federal grants-in-aid are excluded from state and local receipts. All subsequent calculations based on the national income accounts include these two adjustments. Cf. table 2.1.

2. While the "other taxes" category accounts for 28 percent of state and local revenues, no particular item raises over $51.8 billion, the amount generated by the individual income tax.

3. In the national income accounts, the percentage of receipts raised through the corporate tax is 7.7 percent, greater than the number shown in the text due to the inclusion of the profits of the Federal Reserve System.

4. These estimates, based on current tax laws and rates of economic growth and inflation consistent with the administration's budgetary estimates, were made available to us for this study.

5. There does not seem to have been an extensive discussion of these issues in the recent literature. A concise presentation is given in A. B. Atkinson and J. E. Stiglitz, *Lectures in Public Economics* (New York: McGraw-Hill, 1980), lecture 9. For an earlier and extensive criticism of empirical incidence analysis, see A. R. Prest, "Statistical Calculations of Tax Burdens," *Economica* 22 (1955): 234–245, and "The Budget and Interpersonal Distribution," *Public Finance* 23 (1968): 80–98. For a review of literature

through 1980, see George F. Break, "The Incidence and Economic Effects of Taxation," in *Economics of Public Finance* (Washington, D.C.: Brookings, 1974).

6. This example assumes that all dollars are expressed in real terms.

7. Richard Musgrave, *The Theory of Public Finance* (New York: McGraw-Hill, 1959).

8. This seems plausible in the case of labor income, except for those few individuals, such as doctors and lawyers, who have more control over the supply of their services and the prices they charge for them. On the other hand this assumption is much more problematic in the case of income from capital.

9. Detailed assumptions made by Pechman and Okner, on whose updated computations we rely heavily, are reported in their book *Who Bears the Tax Burden?* (Washington, D.C.: Brookings, 1974).

10. Ibid., and Benjamin Okner, "Total U.S. Taxes and Their Effect on the Distribution of Income," in Henry Aaron and Michael Boskin, *The Economics of Taxation* (Washington, D.C.: Brookings, 1980).

11. The 1985 estimates also assume moderate real growth and inflation rates consistent with the administration's current budgetary projections.

12. Pechman and Okner, *Who Bears the Tax Burden?*

13. For details, see ibid.

14. For most lower-income classes, the estimated effective tax rates are higher than for the $5,000–$10,000 group, but these results reflect the large number of families with an annual income well below its normal level.

15. The effect of the reduction in federal income tax rates under the Reagan administration was at least partially offset by bracket creep and an increase in state income taxes.

16. The bottom decile figure shown is actually that for the sixth to tenth percentiles. The figure for the first to fifth percentiles is even higher.

17. One other factor that might be expected to affect the estimated progressivity of the Pechman-Okner estimates is their

omission from income and taxes of receipts of and payments on gifts and bequests because of data inadequacies. However, Pechman and Okner, *Who Bears the Tax Burden?* do present for 1966 rough estimates of tax incidence reflecting such receipts and payments, which suggest that the overall effect of this adjustment is small. Progressivity is reduced under the most progressive incidence assumptions but increased somewhat under the least progressive assumptions.

18. The estimated benefits under such programs by income quintiles have been published for 1970. Okner, "Total U.S. Taxes."

19. Patricia Ruggles and Michael O. Higgins, "The Distribution of Public Expenditures among Households in the United States," *Review of Income and Wealth* (June 1981). Prior to adjustment for nontax fiscal effects, this study points to a more regressive overall tax structure for the 1969–1970 period than the corresponding Pechman-Okner figures. The Ruggles-Higgins results seem to overstate the tax ratio substantially (estimated as 55.3 percent for all income groups combined), apparently a result of their understatement of income.

20. Ruggles and Higgins, "Distribution," provide data for allocating government expenditures by family income. To allocate roughly by net worth, we assumed an average net-worth-to-income ratio of 4.14 for all income groups combined and a ratio of 9.88 for the top decile. These ratios, admittedly rough, are mainly based on estimates of the size distribution of wealth for 1969 by Edward Wolff, and for 1962–1963 by Friend and Blume. The Wolff estimates for the top (open-end) income bracket had to be supplemented by income data from U.S. Internal Revenue Service, *Statistics of Income, 1969: Individual Income Tax Returns* (September 1971).

21. Harvey Galper and Eric Toder, "Measuring the Incidence of Taxation of Income from Capital," Brookings Technical Series, reprint T-026 (Washington, D.C.: Brookings, 1983). However, the Galper-Toder analysis assumes certainty of outcomes. Under uncertainty even the direction of the effect of this adjustment is not clear. See Irwin Friend and Joel Hasbrouck, "Inflation and the Stock Market: Comment," *American Economic Review* (March 1982).

22. The inclusion of nominal interest payments and other nominal returns of capital in the Pechman-Okner estimates of income

also raises questions in an inflationary period, but it is not clear whether an appropriate adjustment would increase or decrease their estimates of the progressivity of taxes.

23. It can be argued that it would be preferable to use actual market data to estimate real capital gains, though this raises other problems.

24. Irwin Friend and Joel Hasbrouck, "The Effect of Inflation on the Profitability and Valuation of U.S. Corporations," in *Savings, Investment and Capital Markets in an Inflationary Economy,* ed. Marshall Sarnat and Giorgio P. Szego (Cambridge, Mass.: Ballinger, 1982). Stock prices in inflationary periods also can be adversely affected by increases in the real required rates of return.

25. An independent check on the Pechman-Okner results is provided by estimates of the tax burden in 1968 by Richard Musgrave, Karl Case, and Herman Leonard, "The Distribution of Fiscal Burdens and Benefits," *Public Finance Quarterly* (July 1974). Their estimates of progressiveness in the tax burden (based on their benchmark assumptions) are closer to the Pechman-Okner least progressive than to the Pechman-Okner most progressive results in 1966 or 1970. Thus Musgrave, Case, and Leonard under their benchmark assumptions estimate that as of 1968 the tax burden rose from 28.5 percent in their under-$4,000 total income class to 35.9 percent in their over-$92,000 total income class. However, if a different measure of net budget incidence is used—benefits net of taxes paid as a percentage of total income—benefits exceed taxes for income brackets under $10,400 and are less than taxes for the higher-income groups. While the ratio of net benefits to income decreases markedly with rising income in the under-$10,400 group, the ratio of net taxes to income increases only modestly with incomes rising above $12,500. The assumptions required for the allocation of a high proportion of benefits to income groups are rather arbitrary.

26. These estimates are obtained from Irwin Friend and Marshall Blume, "The Demand for Risky Assets," *American Economic Review* (December 1975). They are based on data reported in the 1962 and 1963 Federal Reserve Board Surveys of the Financial Characteristics of Consumers and Changes in Family Finances. Independent estimates by Edward Wolff, "The Size Distribution of Household Disposable Wealth in the United States," *Review of*

Income and Wealth (June 1983), point to an increase in the house-hold-wealth-to-income ratio for 1969 from 3.9 in the $5,000–7,499 income bracket to 7.3 in the $50,000–99,999 bracket. These estimates are based on the matching of a large sample survey of families in 1969 with census and Internal Revenue Service data. Somewhat more recent estimates by Daphne Greenwood, "An Estimation of U.S. Family Wealth and Its Distribution from Micro Data, 1973," *Review of Income and Wealth* (March 1983), indicate that when households are classified by wealth percentiles, the net worth–income ratios increased from about one-half in the 41–50 percentile group to four to five in the 91–95 percentile group and about nine in the top percentile group.

27. Eugene Steuerle, "Wealth, Realized Income and the Measure of Well-Being," (National Bureau of Economic Research, Conference on Research in Income and Wealth, December 8–9, 1983).

28. U.S. Department of Labor, Bureau of Labor Statistics, *Consumer Expenditures Survey: Integrated Diary and Interview Survey Data, 1972–73*, bulletin 1992 (Washington, D.C.: Government Printing Office, 1978). The multivariate relation among different socioeconomic demographic characteristics and consumption is not available from this survey. A substantial amount of such information for an earlier period, which if updated would be highly useful in estimating the distributional effects of a consumption tax on different population groups, is available for the Bureau of Labor Statistics 1950 survey. See Jean Crockett and Irwin Friend, "A Complete Set of Consumer Demand Relationships," in Irwin Friend and Robert Jones, eds., *Consumption and Saving* (Philadelphia: University of Pennsylvania, 1960), vol. 1.

29. The consumption ratios adjusted to national income totals were estimated by John Green, "The Effects of Alternative Personal Tax Rate Structures on Savings and Investment" (Ph.D. diss., University of Pennsylvania, 1984).

30. See Irwin Friend and Stanley Schor, "Who Saves?" *Review of Economics and Statistics* (May 1959); Helen Humes Lamale, *Methodology of the Survey of Consumer Expenditures in 1950, Study of Consumer Expenditures, Incomes and Savings* (Philadelphia: University of Pennsylvania, 1959); and Franco Modigliani and Albert Ando, "Hypothesis of Saving Behavior: Comparison and Tests," *Study of Consumer Expenditures, Income and Savings* (Philadelphia: University of Pennsylvania, 1959).

31. Pechman and Okner, *Who Bears the Tax Burden?*

32. See *Consumer Expenditures Survey*.

33. In *Federal Tax Policy*, Brookings Institution Studies of Government Finance (New York: W. W. Norton, 1971), Pechman calculates the effective average tax rates as a percentage of reported income without inventory valuation and capital consumption adjustments, and shows much lower percentages than given in the text; however, the trend in both sets of numbers is the same.

Chapter 3

1. Even the diversifiable part of risk for human wealth, which might be covered by life insurance, involves transaction costs much greater than for most nonhuman wealth.

2. In the early 1970s the progressivity of the U.S. tax structure was not much different from that in other OECD countries for which data were available, except for Sweden where the tax structure was much more progressive and, jointly with transfers and other government expenditures, had a significantly greater redistribution effect. Peter Saunders, *Evidence on Income Redistribution by Government*, working paper no. 11 (Paris, France: OECD Economics and Statistics Department, January 1984).

3. A small number of supply-side economists might question this assessment, but it is supported by all the scientific evidence of which we are aware, including a number of studies referred to in this book, and by the enormous deficits associated with the recent experiment in supply-side economics involving substantial reductions in taxes on both labor and capital income.

4. This is true of marginal as well as average tax rates.

5. The theoretical assumptions under which the optimal tax on capital income is zero are discussed in Alan J. Auerbach, *The Taxation of Capital Income* (Cambridge: Harvard University Press, 1983). Alan J. Auerbach, Lawrence J. Kotlikoff, and Jonathan Skinner, "The Efficiency Gains from Dynamic Tax Reforms," *International Economic Review* (February 1983), shows that while under the assumptions they make consumption taxes result in efficiency gains, these arise chiefly from the placement of large marginal tax burdens on the relatively inelastic elderly.

6. A recent analysis of the relevant evidence is provided in Irwin Friend and Joel Hasbrouck, "Saving and After-Tax Rates of Return," *Review of Economics and Statistics* (November 1983). The relationship between aggregate and private saving associated with changes in capital income taxation will depend on the nature of the transition in the focus of taxation. See Martin Feldstein, "The Rate of Return, Taxation and Personal Saving," *Economic Journal* (September 1978).

7. Proponents of life-cycle or permanent income theories of consumption and saving behavior generally would consider such effects to be short-lived.

8. A rise in the corporate saving-income ratio probably would be partly offset by a decline in the household saving-income ratio, reflecting lower direct saving by stockholders, but, except perhaps in the very long run as higher corporate saving is associated with higher household wealth, it is unlikely that the offset will be anywhere near complete. See Martin S. Feldstein, "Tax Incentives, Corporate Saving and Capital Accumulation in the United States," *Journal of Public Economics* 2 (1973); Martin Feldstein and George Fane, "Taxes, Corporate Dividend Policy and Personal Saving: The British Postwar Experience," *Review of Economics and Statistics* (November 1973); J. Ernest Tanner, "Fiscal Policy and Consumer Behavior," *Review of Economics and Statistics* (May 1979); and E. Philip Howrey and Saul H. Hymans, "The Measurement and Determination of Loanable-Funds Saving," Brookings Papers in Economic Activity 3 (Washington, D.C.: Brookings, 1978).

9. This evidence includes the results obtained from corporate surveys of investment behavior, as well as econometric models based on time-series data. See Marshall Blume, Jean Crockett, and Irwin Friend, "Stimulation of Capital Formation: Ends and Means," in *Toward a New U.S. Industrial Policy*, ed. Michael Wachter and Susan Wachter (Philadelphia: University of Pennsylvania Press, 1981), and several relevant papers in Henry J. Aaron and Joseph A. Pechman, eds., *How Taxes Affect Economic Behavior* (Washington, D.C.: Brookings, 1981).

10. See Marshall Blume and Irwin Friend, *The Effect of a Reduction in Corporate Taxes on Investments in Riskfree and Risky Assets*, working paper 3-84 (Philadelphia: Rodney White Center for Financial

Research, University of Pennsylvania, 1984), for the effect of corporate income taxes, and Irwin Friend and Joel Hasbrouck, "Comment on Inflation and the Stock Market," *American Economic Review* (March 1982), for the effect of personal income taxes. Although theory does not point to a clear negative effect of higher personal income taxes on investment and stock prices, it is frequently stated that such taxes do affect risky investment adversely, especially for small enterpreneurs, but relevant evidence does not seem to be available.

11. The empirical information available includes survey, econometric cross-section and time-series analysis, and social experiments (such as the New Jersey–Pennsylvania income maintenance experiment). See *Taxation and Incentives* (Bath, England: Institute for Fiscal Studies, Mandip Press, 1976); *Theoretical and Empirical Aspects of the Effects of Taxation on the Supply of Labor* (Paris, France: OECD, 1975); and Jerry A. Hausman, "Taxes and Labor Supply," working paper no. 1102 (Washington, D.C.: National Bureau of Economic Research, March 1983). Other relevant qualitative data include the low labor productivity of workers in Communist countries with no economic incentives for maintaining or increasing output. There is reason to believe that this effect may be quite marked, which may reflect a substantial sensitivity of effective labor supply to the provision of some labor incentives but a much smaller effect of increased incentives thereafter.

12. The marked decline from 1950 to 1980 in the percentage of the aged who worked suggests that the accelerated growth of social security and private pension plans had a substantial negative effect on the labor supply.

13. Mervyn A. King and Don Fullerton, "The Taxation of Income from Capital: A Comparative Study of the U.S., U.K., Sweden and West Germany—Comparisons of Effective Tax Rates," working paper no. 1073 (Washington, D.C.: National Bureau of Economic Research, February 1983).

14. The substitution of consumption for income taxes would tend to shift economic output out of the market sector since consumption activities carried out in the home would be subject to no tax or to a lower tax.

15. Cf. chapter 2.

16. Auerbach suggests that safe-harbor leasing that allowed the transfer of tax benefits from one corporation to another may have reduced this distortion.

17. A. C. Harberger, "The Corporation Income Tax: An Empirical Appraisal," in *Tax Revision Compendium* (Washington, D.C.: Government Printing Office, 1959), Vol. 1, "The Incidence of the Corporation Income Tax," *Journal of Political Economy* 70 (June 1962), and "Efficiency Effects of Taxes on Income from Capital," in *Effects of Corporation Income Tax*, ed. M. Krzyzaniak (Detroit: Wayne State University Press, 1966).

18. John Shoven, "The Incidence of Efficiency Effects of Taxes on Income from Capital," *Journal of Political Economy* 84 (1976), redid Harberger's work, correcting a mathematical error and what he considers a conceptual error. The result was a slightly smaller estimate than Harberger's.

19. Idem.

20. Auerbach calculates the distortion as a percentage of the total capital stock. As such it appears to be a big number, but expressed as an equivalent annuity it is comparable to earlier estimates of lost income as a percentage of GNP.

21. Shoven, "Incidence."

22. Joel Slemrod and Nikki Sorum, "The Compliance Cost of the U.S. Individual Income Tax System" (Minneapolis: University of Minnesota, February 1984); and Joel Slemrod, "The Return to Tax Simplification: An Econometric Analysis" (Minneapolis: University of Minnesota, December 1983).

23. The total cost of the U.S. Internal Revenue Service in fiscal 1983 was a little over $3.0 billion. Prepared statement by Joseph A. Minarik, *The Flat Tax Rate*, Hearings before the Subcommittee on Monetary and Fiscal Policy of the Joint Economics Committee, July 27, 1982.

24. Ibid.

25. This is not quite true. Most federal excise taxes (on gasoline and oil, tobacco and alcoholic beverages) are specific taxes rather than ad valorem taxes. For this reason federal excise tax revenues fall significantly in real terms, and hence they are somewhat pro-

cyclical. There is little justification for this situation, and these taxes should be reformulated as ad valorem taxes.

26. Undistributed profits since 1979, the last year before the subsequent recession, moved as follows: 1979, $112 billion; 1980, $91 billion; 1981, $80 billion; 1982, $46 billion; 1983, $56 billion.

27. Martin Feldstein, "Inflation, Tax Rates and the Stock Market," *Journal of Monetary Economics* (July 1980), and Friend and Hasbrouck, "Comment on Inflation and the Stock Market."

28. Joel Hasbrouck, "Impact of Inflation upon Corporate Taxation," *National Tax Journal* (March 1983).

29. A study by the New York Stock Exchange, *An Analysis of the Capital Gains Holding Period* (New York: Office of Economic Research, July 1982) notes that there is a negative (cross-section) correlation between effective tax rates on realized capital gains and the personal saving rate for eight countries. This is not strong evidence of a causal relationship, however, and may be contrasted with the positive correlation between capital income taxation and capital formation for four of these countries.

30. The degree of stimulation will depend on the nature of the reduction in corporate taxes and especially on the extent to which it is applicable to marginal rather than average investment.

31. See Friend and Hasbrouck, "Comment on Inflation and the Stock Market," for some of the difficulties in determining the theoretically expected impact of capital gains taxation on stock prices. Joseph E. Stiglitz, "Some Aspects of the Taxation of Capital Gains," working paper no. 1094 (Washington, D.C.: National Bureau of Economic Research, March 1983), shows that on theoretical grounds a reduction in capital gains taxes or a shortening in the holding period can either increase or decrease saving.

32. Thus Roger E. Brinner and Stephen H. Brooks, "Stock Prices," in Aaron and Pechman, eds., *How Taxes Affect Economic Behavior*, find an insignificant capital gains tax effect on stock prices—with the wrong sign.

33. It has even been argued that the discouragement of short-term realization of capital gains is economically desirable as a means of reducing market speculation, but there is no strong theoretical or empirical support for this position.

34. For example, see Joseph J. Minarik, Martin Feldstein, Joel Slemrod, and Shlomo Yitzhaki, "The Effects of Taxation on the Selling of Corporate Stock and the Realization of Capital Gains," *Quarterly Journal of Economics* (February 1984); comments on the effect of capital gains taxation by John Yinger, William D. Nordhaus, Joseph Minarik, and Martin Feldstein in *Tax Notes,* October 30, December 4, 1978; April 5, May 2, May 9, 1983; and Gerald E. Auten, "The Taxation of Capital Gains," mimeo. (Bowling Green State University, December 1982).

35. Stiglitz, "Some Aspects," considers on theoretical grounds that while a lowering of the tax rate of long-term capital gains might lead to increased realization of capital gains and increased government revenues in the short run, in the long run it is likely to decrease government revenues. He also shows "in a perfect capital market, there are no real consequences of capital gains taxation; while in an imperfect capital market, there may or may not be a locked-in effect." In an empirical analysis of a panel of taxpayers, Gerald E. Auten and Charles T. Clotfelter, "Permanent versus Transitory Tax Effects and the Realization of Capital Gains," *Quarterly Journal of Economics* (November 1982), find that it is not clear whether permanent cuts in capital gains taxes would increase or reduce tax revenues.

36. At the state level taxes on investment income are sometimes levied indirectly as some form of wealth tax.

37. For a detailed discussion of estate and gift taxes, see J. Kurtz and S. Surrey, "Reform of Death and Gift Taxes: 1968 Treasury Proposals, the Criticisms, and a Rebuttal," *Columbia Law Review* 70 (1970).

38. This amount of $3.1 million is the sum of the $600,000, the exemption equivalent amount, and $2.5 million, the transfer in excess of the exemption equivalent amount.

39. These percentages would be reduced to the extent of any state death credits and foreign death credits. As noted by Harvey Galper, "The Coming Reexamination of Tax Policy," *Tax Notes,* May 2, 1983, the actual tax collection from estate and gift taxes has "never bulked large in the U.S. tax structure, and the avenues of escape from these taxes are well known and widely used. Nonetheless, the 1981 act will greatly decrease this tax, cutting revenues in 1986 from $11.5 billion to $5.0 billion and

(assuming 1982 wealth levels) reducing the number of taxable estates from 2.8% of decedents to 0.3% when the law is fully effective. Even estates of fairly substantial size ($600,000 in 1987 and subsequent years) can avoid tax completely."

Chapter 4

1. For a detailed discussion of the 1963–1965 act and its effects, see, for instance, Joseph A. Pechman, "Individual Income Tax Provisions of the Revenue Act of 1964," *Journal of Finance* (May 1965): 247–272.

2. One other factor, the standard deduction, plays a role similar to personal exemptions in this context. It is difficult to describe the role the standard deduction played during this period, primarily for two reasons. (1) In 1955 the standard deduction was the minimum of 10 percent of adjusted gross income or $1,000 ($500 for married persons filing separately) (U.S. Internal Revenue Service, *Statistics of Income, Individual Returns 1955*, p. 85); in 1981 it was a flat $2,300 for single individuals and $3,400 for married couples filing jointly. Since in 1981 per capita personal income was some 5.6 times that for 1955, the 1955 provision scaled to the per capita personal income of 1981 would say that the standard deduction should be 10 percent of adjusted gross income or $5,600, whichever is smaller. It is difficult to compare these two provisions. One might say that the aggregate effect is roughly similar, although the current provision is relatively more progressive for the lower-income groups. (2) There are movements back and forth by taxpayers between standard and itemized deductions, and we cannot account for these shifts easily. In spite of these difficulties, we believe it is within reason for our present purposes to suppose that the effects of standard deduction remained roughly the same in 1955 and 1981 for taxpayers as a whole.

3. For a more detailed history of the relationship between taxable income and personal income, see Pechman, *Federal Tax Policy*, p. 63, appendix B.

4. This assumption is roughly correct for all income classes other than the lower-income groups.

5. Here we use personal income as defined by national income

accounts as the starting point, although it does not include capital gains and losses and therefore is somewhat defective.

6. The discussion of progressivity in this chapter refers to the individual income tax system and not to the total effect of the fiscal activities of the government. When transfer payments are taken into account, the lowest income group, especially elderly members of that group, are better off than indicated by the considerations of the tax system alone. Once the expenditure side of the government fiscal activities is introduced into the discussion, the distributional effects of all federal expenditures, rather than those of the transfer system alone, should be considered.

7. This is because a given amount of deduction reduces the tax liability of a taxpayer more and more as his or her marginal tax rate increases, while a given amount of credit reduces the tax liability of a taxpayer by a constant amount independent of the marginal rate he faces.

8. Low-income groups are protected by the wider zero tax bracket or larger tax credits.

9. The current level of progressivity of the overall tax system is one in which broad income groups are taxed at roughly a constant ratio of their income. See chapter 2 for details.

10. There exists one precedent of a refundable credit: earned income credit under the current tax code. If the adjusted gross income and the earned income of a taxpayer are each less than $10,000, the taxpayer may be entitled to an earned income credit of up to $500. If the taxpayer's gross tax liability is less than his or her earned income credit, the taxpayer is entitled to the refund for the difference.

11. The distribution of wealth is known to be more concentrated than the distribution of income.

12. U.S. Department of Treasury, *Blueprints for Basic Tax Reform* (Washington, D.C.: Government Printing Office, January 17, 1977).

13. The estimate of the total tax expenditure of $239.3 billion for 1983 reported by the Joint Committee on Taxation does not include the tax expenditure associated with failure to tax unrealized capital gains.

14. More specifically the amount of the benefit subject to tax will be the lesser of one-half of the benefits received or one-half of the excess of the combined income over the base amount. The combined income is modified adjusted gross income plus one-half of social security benefits. Modified adjusted gross income is adjusted gross income plus any tax-exempt interest received; plus deduction for a married couple when both work; plus excluded amounts earned abroad, in U.S. possessions, or in Puerto Rico. The base amount is $32,000 if the filing status is married filing jointly, zero if it is married filing separately while living with his or her spouse at any time during the year, and $25,000 for any other filing status.

15. Treasury, *Blueprints*.

16. Major ones are the Fair Tax Act of 1983 sponsored by Senator Bill Bradley and Congressman Richard A. Gephardt (H.R. 3271); the Fair and Simple Tax Act of 1984 sponsored by Congressman Jack F. Kemp and Senator Bob Kasten (H.R. 5533); one proposed by Senator Dennis DeConcini (S. 557); and the SELF Tax Plan Act of 1983 sponsored by Senator Dan Quayle (S. 1040).

17. Some major differences between the K-K proposal and the B-G proposal, in addition to differences in the rate schedule and the size of exemptions and standard deductions, are: the K-K proposal allows all deductions to be subtracted for computation on all taxes, while the B-G proposal allows the deductions for computation of the regular taxes at 14 percent but not for computation of surtaxes; some tax expenditure items, such as interest payments on personal loans, are retained in the K-K proposal but not in the B-G proposal; and the B-G proposal would include all realized capital gains in the tax base, without indexing, while the K-K proposal would allow the taxpayer to elect, on a year-by-year basis, a 25 percent exclusion on the proposed indexing of capital gains for a transition period of ten years.

18. A proposal discussed recently, in which state and local governments were to be given the option of retaining the right to issue tax-exempt bonds or to renounce the right to do so in return for a subsidy by the federal government, would retain the undesirable features of the current tax law from the viewpoints of economic efficiency and equity while increasing the federal expenditure.

19. Since, under the B-G proposal, all capital gains would be taxed at the ordinary rate, this rule is roughly equivalent to letting

the donor deduct the gift at market value, then requiring that any implied capital gain on a basis of the depreciated acquisition cost be included in the tax base of the donor, while any implied capital loss is not allowed to affect his or her tax base. The reason for excluding capital losses from the tax base is to avoid potential tax shelters. The donor always has the option of selling the asset, realizing the loss, and donating the proceeds to the charity. The Internal Revenue Service would be instructed to prepare a depreciation schedule for some broad categories of assets and to require the depreciation of all other items at some uniform rate, say at a straight line depreciation schedule over ten years.

20. See, for example, the release from Senator Bradley's office dated April 14, 1983.

21. The indexing scheduled to become effective under the current law in 1985 merely refers to marginal tax bracket definitions, personal exemptions, and standard deductions; it is only a small fraction of total indexing outlined in the text. The consequences of such a partial indexing are difficult to predict, and it would be difficult to determine whether it is beneficial or harmful to the economy.

22. One important problem with the CPI is that it reflects relative changes of prices in domestically produced and imported goods; that is, when the price of imports rises relative to the cost of domestic production, the CPI rises. An attempt to adjust all domestic prices proportionately to changes in import prices can lead to uncontrollable inflationary pressures. For the United States this may not be as serious a problem as for those countries for which foreign trade is a much larger proportion of the net domestic product. A somewhat less accurate solution—that adjustments be based on CPI or the average wage rate change, whichever is less—may be quite satisfactory under most conditions in the United States. Another rule mentioned in policy discussions is to index the tax system by the rate of change in CPI less 2 percent or so. This type of adjustment of the CPI is sometimes justified on the grounds that the CPI for technical reasons tends to overstate the rate of inflation or that there is an advantage in providing households with some incentive to support anti-inflation measures. Note, however, that it can cause difficulties, for instance, when domestic value-added prices rise more rapidly than raw materials prices. Either one of these two

approximate rules would have been an improvement over the prevailing system during the 1970s, though it would have left the tax system with a moderate inflation bias.

23. This problem may be somewhat less serious than it appears. If the market rate of interest remains the same before and after the tax reform, the problem would be fairly severe. But the market rate of interest will not remain the same. Almost certainly the monetary authorities would allow the market rate of interest to decline in the face of such a major increase in the cost of borrowing due to a tax revision, especially if the elimination of tax incentives for investment on productive business capital is undertaken at the same time. Home owners, particularly low- to middle-income home owners, may find that the net costs of their mortgages do not increase significantly. This is true of those purchasing new homes and those who have variable rate mortgages, but home owners with fixed rate mortgages may still face the difficulty, although this too may not be too severe since most mortgage contracts allow early repayment after a short initial period. Even so it may be advisable for the tax revision to include some provision for an orderly recontracting of mortgages for those with fixed rate mortgages. The alleviation of these transitory problems does not imply that the inherent effects of the reform, some shifts of the tax burden from renters to home owners, would or should be eliminated.

24. A careful statement of this idea appears in Michael J. Graetz, "The 1982 Minimum Tax Amendments as a First Step in the Transition to a 'Flat Rate' Tax," *Southern California Law Review* (January 1983).

25. Further information is required to ensure that it would be possible to carry out this reform without a significant upward revision in the top marginal tax rate under the B-G proposal. Note, however, that employer contributions are already excluded from the tax base of the employer, and therefore the proposed change would make only the employee contributions deductible, and only for computing the standard tax, not the surtax; and although a substantial portion of benefits would still be excluded from the tax base because of personal exemptions and standard deductions, some of them would be taxed at surtax rates under the B-G tax structure.

If political considerations require that benefits be made fully taxable only when those individuals whose contributions are allowed to be deductible for income tax purposes become eligible for benefits, then there may be substantial loss of revenue for the government for a fairly extended period of time. This situation could be mitigated by first extending the current rule, under which half of social security benefits is included in the tax base for only those taxpayers with a relatively large amount of income from other sources, to all taxpayers. This change should not cause any substantial hardship to beneficiaries with no other sources of income since they would be protected through personal exemptions and standard deductions. The proportion of benefits to be included in the tax base could then be increased gradually over time; at the same time the deduction of only a fraction of employee contributions could initially be allowed, which can then be increased gradually over time, finally leading to the system described in the text.

26. By including the following items, it would be possible to broaden the tax base even further than envisioned by the B-G proposal: all capital gains, realized or unrealized, at death in the tax base, or substantial strengthening of the current law on estate and gift taxation; the interest received from newly issued state and local general obligation bonds in the tax base; and the benefits from the old age and survivor's insurance system in the individual income tax base and allowing the deduction of employee contributions to this program from that base. The proposal might also be improved through the following incorporation of well-constructed and thorough indexing provisions into the tax system to allow for general price level changes and the substitution of a smoother, gradually progressive marginal rate schedule for the one envisioned in the B-G proposal, retaining the same zero tax bracket and top marginal rate.

Chapter 5

1. In their most progressive assumptions of tax incidence, Pechman and Okner, *Who Bears the Tax Burden?* allocate one-half of the burden of the corporate income taxes to stockholders and one-half to property owners in general. In their least progressive assumptions, they allocate one-half to consumers and one-half to property owners in general.

2. A somewhat related argument sometimes made is that corporate profits representing the excess of net current receipts over all current costs, including the cost of capital, can be regarded as a quasi-monopolistic or noncompetitive return that might properly be subjected to a separate tax. There is, of course, no easy way to distinguish between competitive and noncompetitive returns.

3. Alan J. Auerbach and other economists, however, have suggested that under present law corporate income in practice may be taxed "essentially once, regardless of the form it takes: debt is taxed at the personal level, equity at the corporate level (ignoring the relatively lightly taxed individual capital gains)." See Auerbach, "Welfare Aspects of Current U.S. Corporate Taxation," *American Economic Review* (May 1983). According to this view the personal tax on dividends exerts no marginal effect on corporate investment behavior as long as retained earnings serve as the source of equity funds. The basic reason for this conclusion is that a dollar of new investment is predicated to raise the firm's market value by less than a dollar so that the personal tax gains from avoiding the payment of dividends is offset by a decline in stock prices.

4. Another criticism of corporate income taxes frequently heard in the 1950s and 1960s was that such taxes tended to have an adverse effect on the U.S. balance of payments, but this argument loses much of its potency with a system of flexible exchange rates under which the world has operated since 1973. (See Pechman, *Federal Tax Policy*.)

5. John B. Shoven and Paul Taubman, "Saving, Capital Income and Taxation," in Henry J. Aaron and Michael J. Boskin, eds., *The Economics of Taxation* (Washington, D.C.: Brookings, 1980), describe a full integration scenario in which there would be only a moderate loss in total tax revenue.

6. Alan J. Auerbach, "Corporate Taxation in the United States," Brookings Papers on Economic Activity 2 (Washington, D.C.: Brookings, 1983).

7. Historical data on the relative importance of corporate taxes back to 1953 are provided in ibid., pp. 256, 453. Also see tables 2.6 and 2.12 in this book.

8. The substantial reduction over recent years in the rate of taxation on income from capital generally, relative to the taxation on

income from labor, has been commented on earlier. See tables 2.11, 2.12.

9. Auerbach, "Corporate Taxation," p. 471.

10. Ibid.

11. U.S. Department of Commerce, *Survey of Current Business* (January 1984), pp. 16, 22.

12. Auerbach, "Corporate Taxation," p. 497.

13. This line of reasoning, if applied to individuals instead of corporations, would imply that a decline in personal tax rates is associated with the cancellation of implicit debt to the government. The amount cancelled would be equal to the present value of the decrease in the future flow of such taxes. Human wealth, of course, is not marketable so that there are no measurable capital gains involved.

14. It is not clear how a substantial reduction in or elimination of corporate income taxes would affect the perceived riskiness of stock and hence the required after-tax rate of return, but if there is any resulting offsetting effect on stock prices, it is likely to be relatively small.

15. The procedures followed are designed to equate approximately the present value of depreciation deductions and the present value of economic depreciation at a 10 percent discount rate. Implicit in these procedures is an assumed inflation rate of about 6 percent. Memorandum by Joe Minarik to Senator Bill Bradley and Congressman Richard Gephardt, "Depreciation in the Bradley-Gephardt Proposal," April 14, 1983.

16. The $43.8 billion of tax revenues resulting from the repeal of most corporate tax expenditures under current law may be compared with a total of corporate tax expenditures of $56.7 billion according to Joint Committee on Taxation–Congressional Budget Office estimates (appendix A). The largest difference between these two figures is accounted for by the retention in Bradley-Gephardt of the close to $7.0 billion exclusion of interest on general purpose state and local government debt.

17. The depressant effect on housing would be justified by some economists either as an offset to the preferential treatment of housing in other provisions of current tax law or as a judgment

that plant and equipment expenditures are more important for productivity and overall economic welfare.

18. Marshall E. Blume, Irwin Friend and Randolph Westerfield, *Impediments to Capital Formation* (Philadelphia: Rodney L. White Center for Financial Research, Wharton School, University of Pennsylvania, December 1980). Of course, if saving is relatively unresponsive to interest rates, the effectiveness of any investment incentives on total investment would depend on their impact on the real level of the national income.

19. Auerbach, "Corporate Taxation," pp. 470 ff.

20. Neither Bradley-Gephardt nor this book addresses directly the important but complex questions relating to the desirability of eliminating the corporate tax preferences provided for debt capital and to the major transitional problems raised by such a change. However, the full integration of corporate and personal taxes discussed in the next section would eliminate the preferential treatment of corporate debt and the associated adverse effects on investment decisions, though as noted subsequently there will be substantial transitional problems in the process of achieving such integration.

21. Treasury, *Blueprints*, p. 200.

22. For previously issued tax-exempt bonds, such a grandfathering argument might be more persuasive.

23. Treasury, *Blueprints*, p. 186, states that the immediate asset price changes would be greater for long-term fixed claims than for equity investments, but it is not at all clear that this would generally be true. For example, the elimination of some of their preferential treatment would lower the relative prices of the new municipals affected in this manner but raise the relative prices of municipals issued in the pre-Bradley-Gephardt period. Bonds of companies adversely affected by a reduction in the preferential tax treatment of the issuer would be expected to be less affected than corporate equities by the B-G tax changes.

24. Several approaches have been proposed for this purpose: the adjustment of historical cost depreciation on the basis of replacement cost for individual capital assets or groups of assets; adjustment of historical costs on the basis of movements in the general price level; and allowance of an immediate deduction for the

present value of future economic depreciation in the absence of inflation. Pechman, *Federal Tax Policy*.

25. Auerbach, "Corporate Taxation," points out that an appropriate economic solution for losses is to permit unlimited carryforwards with interest. Provision for refundable taxes would be another appropriate economic solution but raises a greater danger of fraudulent tax loss claims.

26. Friend and Hasbrouck, "Effect of Inflation."

27. More serious reservations could be raised about the present version of the Kemp-Kasten flat tax (S. 2600) since its enactment would significantly raise the capital gains to stockholders associated with the reduction in the statutory corporate tax rates to 30 percent while retaining accelerated depreciation.

28. The main methods used at various times in different countries are described in Pechman, *Federal Tax Policy*.

29. How significant the revenue loss would be would depend on the treatment of currently tax-exempt institutions and foreigners.

30. Joseph A. Pechman, "Tax Policies for the 1980s," in Pechman and Simler, eds., *Economics and the Public Service* (New York: W. W. Norton, 1982), and Alvin Warren, "The Relation and Integration of Individual and Corporate Income Taxes," *Harvard Law Review* (February 1981).

31. Special Committee on Simplification, Section of Taxation, American Bar Association, "Evaluation of the Proposed Model Comprehensive Income Tax," *Tax Lawyer* 32 (1979).

32. Ibid., p. 603.

33. Treasury, *Blueprints*, p. 195.

34. If the Bradley-Gephardt or some similar measure is not enacted, eliminating or greatly reducing corporate tax preferences, partial integration would be made much more difficult since dividend relief would presumably require distinctions to be made between dividends paid out of taxed and untaxed corporate earnings.

35. *Federal Income Tax Project, Subchapter C: Proposals on Corporate Aquisitions and Dispositions and Reporter's Study of Corporate Distributions* (American Law Institute, 1982). See especially "Reporter's

Study of the Taxation of Corporate Distributions." Associated with this dividend relief plan for new equity are proposals to impose a flat rate excise tax on nondividend distributions (such as stock repurchases) and to eliminate, in the case of portfolio investment by corporations, the current dividend-received deduction.

36. For further discussion see Warren, "Relation and Integration of Individual and Corporate Income Taxes."

37. The part-year stockholder and the retrospective audit problems referred to previously do not seem serious to us and could be handled in a number of different ways, including the attribution of retained earnings to only end-of-year stockholders relying on stock prices to make the necessary adjustments.

38. *The Structure and Reform of Direct Taxation: Report of a Committee Chaired by Professor J. E. Meade* (Institute for Fiscal Studies, Allen and Unwin, 1978); Treasury, *Blueprints.*

39. Henry J. Aaron and Harvey Galper, "Reforming the Tax System," in Alice M. Rivlin, ed., *Economic Choices 1984* (Washington, D.C.: Brookings, 1984).

40. Aaron and Galper, ibid., p. 98, say of a corporate cash-flow tax, "Deductions for business expenditures on consumption items for the benefit of employees or owners would be denied." A similar treatment of such business expenditures could be required for corporate income tax purposes.

41. A similar conclusion is reached in *Structure and Reform of Direct Taxation.* The Meade committee report spells out several different approaches to the implementation of a corporate cash-flow tax.

Chapter 6

1. Treasury, *Blueprints.*

2. Alan J. Auerbach, et al., "The Efficiency Gains of Dynamic Tax Reform," *International Economic Review* (February 1983); Treasury, *Blueprints*; John E. Chapoton, "Statement of the Honorable John E. Chapoton, Assistant Secretary of the Treasury for Tax Policy, before the Senate Finance Committee," September 28, 1982; Don Fullerton, John B.Shoven, and John Whalley, "Replacing the U.S.

Income Tax with a Progressive Consumption Tax: A Sequenced General Equilibrium Approach," reprint 400 (Washington, D.C.: National Bureau of Economic Research, May 1982); Harvey Galper, "The Coming Reexamination of Tax Policy," Tax Analysts Special Report, *Tax Notes*, May 2, 1983; and *Structure and Reform of Direct Taxation*.

3. Treasury, *Blueprints*; and "Statement of the Honorable John E. Chapoton."

4. Examples include: Charles P. Alexander, "Tax Ideas from Flat to VAT: Looking for Ways to Make the Bite on Income Less Unfair," *Time*, April 16, 1984; and Richard L. Strout, "VAT More Eggs with Less Squawk?" *Christian Science Monitor*, January 28, 1983.

5. *Structure and Reform of Direct Taxation*; Strout, "VAT."

6. Treasury, *Blueprints*.

7. Abstracting from inheritances and assuming that all wealth is consumed just before death, a consumption tax in a sense is equivalent to a proportional wage tax.

8. In an uncertain world a person's future actual wealth can differ greatly from that expected. Sometimes wealth will be greater than expected and sometimes less. The discount rate used in calculating the expected taxes will take this into account. Thus under a flat consumption tax, two households, each with the same initial wealth and the same pattern of future wage income, will face the same present value of expected future consumption. Under a flat consumption tax a household whose wealth turned out to be greater than anticipated would still pay a flat tax on consumption, while under an ability-to-pay tax, the household would pay a tax at a greater average rate than expected. The net result is that a tax based on the ability-to-pay principle is not neutral with respect to consumption but would be regarded as more equitable, according to this principle.

9. Treasury, *Blueprints*.

10. The effect of the tax treatment of defined-benefit plans is much harder to evaluate since it is difficult to allocate the ownership of such plans, and the benefits finally paid are only indirectly related to the value of the fund.

11. Although the literature gives more emphasis to allocating expenses to taxation periods, there is also a difficulty in allocating income.

12. *Structure and Reform of Direct Taxation*, pp. 35–38.

13. Henry J. Aaron, ed., *The Value-Added Tax: Lessons from Europe*, Studies of Government Finance (Washington, D.C.: Brookings, 1981).

14. It could be argued that ultimately there would be no adverse effect on labor incentives since the present value of investments that are consumed in subsequent years is identical to the wages that are saved to produce that future consumption.

15. *The Value-Added Tax: Lessons from Europe.*

16. Ibid. By U.S. standards the costs of collecting the corporate tax are high, roughly four times as great as in the United States.

17. "The Case for Tax Reform," *Economist* (September 1983): 44.

18. Who receives the tax should not be confused with the incidence of the tax.

19. Galper, "Coming Reexamination of Tax Policy," estimated that in 1985 a VAT of 1 percent on half of the potentially taxable consumption goods would yield $10.5 billion. More recently Galper, in Rivlin, *Economic Choices 1984*, estimated that the same tax but in 1989 would yield $18 billion. Assuming that consumption expenditures grow at 10 percent per year, this 1989 estimate is equivalent to $12.3 billion in 1985. These estimates appear reasonable in comparison to the general level of personal consumption expenditures that are likely to prevail in 1985. Moreover we checked Galper's numbers against the 1973 Survey of Consumer Expenditures updated to 1985 using Pechman's numbers presented in chapter 2.

20. In comparison to an income tax, individuals consuming out of prior savings would be worse off by the net increase in tax paid, not by the total consumption tax.

21. If the government wished to raise additional revenues, it could use a VAT or an alternative tax to raise the revenues. In both cases the spending power of consumers is reduced by the same amount. Because other types of taxes would not increase the CPI initially, to neutralize the unique effect of a VAT would

require that the initial increase in the CPI not activate cost of living clauses.

22. Pechman, *Federal Tax Policy*.

23. To maintain the same overall tax incidence as currently, all families would receive some reduction in their marginal rates, but the percentage reduction would decrease with increases in income.

24. In addition under the invoice system, there would be an audit trail to facilitate compliance.

25. Investment assets would include cash balances and other liquid assets.

26. If the present value of the imputed rent is the same as the purchase price of the house, it turns out that the imputed rent is taxed. Treasury, *Blueprints*, presents the theoretical argument.

27. "Case for Tax Reform."

28. Total investment income includes capital gains and losses.

29. Treasury, *Blueprints*, presents an alternative situation in which the inheritance is from a prepaid investment. In this case the tax base may be negative, requiring a large tax refund. *Blueprints* suggests that this type of refund not be given.

30. Committee on Simplification, Section of Taxation, American Bar Association, "Complexity and the Personal Consumption Tax," *Tax Lawyer* 35 (1981–1982): 415–442.

31. The committee did indicate that the proposal would be much simpler if certain types of assets had to be prepaid and the remainder qualified, removing the option of the taxpayer to make the classification. The proposal in "Case for Tax Reform" conforms to this suggestion.

32. For various technical reasons the figure of $1,135.6 billion is probably overstated, but even after correction, it would still be greater than the taxable amount under the current law.

33. In any particular tax period the marginal rates for a consumption tax would be greater than those for an income tax. The effect on incentives should be carefully evaluated. Cf. Shoven and Taubman, "Saving, Capital Income and Taxation."

34. If existing assets were not grandfathered and had to be placed in qualified accounts, taxpayers would have an incentive to underreport their existing assets at the time of transition.

35. It may be possible to realize most of the objectives of this transition rule by requiring only a limited number of taxpayers to calculate the tax under the old system. For example, the transition rules might exempt those taxpayers with an AGI of less than some prespecified amount at the initiation of the new system from calculating the tax under the old system.

36. Treasury, *Blueprints*, p. 210.

37. There would have to be special provisions for closely held corporations.

38. Cf. David Bradford, "Do We Need a Consumption Tax: It's a Fairer Way to Tax the Public," *New York Times*, January 29, 1983.

39. Of course, provisions would have to be made so that taxpayers could not borrow outside their IRAs and use the proceeds to invest in IRAs. This is the same problem present under the current law in the use of borrowed funds to buy municipal bonds and is controlled in part by limitations on the level of interest deductions that is permitted.

Index